THIS CARTOON BOOK IS THE COMBINATION OF TELEVISION NEWS, PROVERBS, IDIOMS, HOMONYMS AND THE THOUGHTS OF 2 BIRDS.

WATCHING NEWS ON T. V. INSPIRED MANY NEWSTOONS: ADDRESSING CITIZENS CONCERNS, THE WINNER IS, BORDER CAPITALISM, SUPPORTING WOMEN, ALWAYS THINKING, WALLA, DACA, CHAINA AND MANY MORE.

CRYING FOWL, GETTING A LEG UP, IT'S NOW A REAR STEAK, LONELY AT THE TOP, PROOFS IN THE PUDDING, SINK YOUR TEETH IN AND MANY MORE WERE CREATED FROM HOMONYMS, PROVERBS AND IDIOMS.

THE 2 BIRDS OFFER INFORMATION AND HUMOR IN BIRDTOONS: ORIGINAL TWEETERS, BLUEBIRD THE PIRATE, GEESE ON GRASS, DON'T LET THE CAT OUT, F. NIGHTINGALE AND NEED 2 WINGS.

THE 101 CARTOONS BOOK DISPLAYS INTERESTING TOONS, RELATED COMMENTARY AND ALSO COMMENTARY NOT RELATED TO THE TOON.

ENJOY THE CARTOON IDEAS AND PUZZLING CLARITY.

101 CARTOONS © 2018   BY J. ASCHER
ALL RIGHTS RESERVED
jerrykeyc@yahoo.com

ABOUT THE TOONOLOGIST, AUTHOR J. ASCHER
101 CARTOONS-BIRDTOONS-NEWSTOONS ---P. C..

WROTE "GAMES OF ATIFACTION"   © 2017
THRIFTEEE--CRAFTEEE--SLEAZEEE--REEEDICULOUS
73 SHORT STORIES ---FEATURING A QUEST FOR $$$,
NOT OFFERED TO THE PUBLIC AS YET.

AUTHOR'S P. C., --- PROUD CONNECTIONS

ARMY NATIONAL GUARD,---PATRIOTIC COMMITMENT

VOLUNTEER COMMUNITY AMBULANCE EMT, PERSONAL CONCERN

GLORY RECORDS 1958, "MARLENE", "WITH YOUR GIRL", PERKY CONTENT--- NOT A BIG SELLER

HARMONICA PERFORMANCES,---PLEASANT COMEDY QUOTED IN THE NEW YORK TIMES.

THIS CARTOON BOOK IS DEDICATED TO THE FIVE WHO CALL ME SILLY SABA. ADA, CDA, E A-V, J A-V, AND L A-V. ALSO TO MY UNCLE IZZY, WHO IS 95, SAYING "I DIDN'T KNOW YOU WERE SMART ENOUGH TO WRITE A BOOK"

I MISS MY SON LARRY WHO IS NOT HERE TO DISCUSS THE CARTOONS WITH ME.

THANKS RHO, FOR COMPUTER TYPING DIRECTION.
THANKS DANIELLE FOR YOUR TECHNICAL EXPERTISE.

INTRODUCTION -------- 101 CARTOONS

Many years ago I was a junior high school math teacher, an English teacher and I supervised a school newspaper. My cartoon ideas, drawn by a student, appeared in each issue. Now as I watch cable news TV, I view much of it as a cartoon.

One day I thought about fooling around with cartoons and titles. After a list of ideas, I felt there could be 100 cartoons and with some writing associated with each cartoon, there could be a book. For some reason, of which I have no recollection, I drew two birds. After repositioning these birds, I saw birds speaking to each other. This led to a number of BIRDTOONS. I liked the birds so much that I named them, BeeKee and BilHorn. Watching cable news gave me ideas for many NEWSTOONS.

This list of NEWS words appear in the cartoons in this book. Border, Business, Capitalism, Chain, Congress, Daca, Debunked, Decisions, Doctor, Flu Shot, Impeachable, Left Wing, Movie Stars, No Fly Zone, Poles, Politicians, Profiling, Protests, Pull Strings, Right Wing, Role Call, Sanctions, Senator, Support, Tax Plan, Tweeters, Vet, Voter, Wall and Women.

This book looks to be politically neutral. No singling out any person or party names. SOME TOONS not labeled NEWSTOONS have a news slant. Much of the writing relates to our daily lives.

The original thought was to have the more difficult TOONS drawn by an artist. But after a couple of contacts the easier option was to scratch them out as good as can do. Many of the CARTOONS relate to sayings, idioms, proverbs, quotes, put into a humorous picture.

Let it be known that this TOONOLOGIST has zero art training. But dad earned his living with his art talent for about 60 years. Dad put on a show painting letters and logos on business windows in Manhattan. Thank you, George; your work was admired.

Try to be open-minded just like the TOONOLOGIST. Enjoy the TOONS and the tongue-in-cheek writing.

TABLE OF CONTENTS ----------101 CARTOONS

1. NEWS, ADDRESSING CONCERNS
2. NEWS, AND THE WINNER IS
3. ANOTHER BALLBUSTER
4. NEWS, ANOTHER USE FOR SHOVELS
5. AUTO BIOGRAPHIES
6. BARE HUNTING
7. BOARD DRY
8. NEWS, BORDER CAPITALISM
9. BIRDS, ORIGINAL TWEETERS
10. BIRDS, NEW TAX PLAN
11. BIRDS, GIVE ME LIBERTY
12. BORED OF EDUCATION
13. BUYING TIME
14. A CHANGE IN THE POLES
15. CITIES ADD JOBS
16. CRYING FOWL
17. DENTIST'S WORK TIME
18. NEWS, DOCTOR, DACA, VOTER
19. A DOG POUND
20. BIRDS, NO BEAK TWEETS
21. BIRDS, PATRIOT DON'T SHOOT
22. BIRDS, BIRDBOOK, BLUEBIRD THE PIRATE
23. NEWS, THE CAN-CAN
24. FINAL SAIL
25. GETTING A LEG UP
26. GETTING RID OF LDL'S
27. NEWS, GREAT WALL OF CHAINA
28. HE BED VETS
29. HOME SCHOOLING
30. HORSE DRAWN WAGON
31. BIRDS, FAMOUS PEOPLE TWEET
32. BIRDS, KILLING BIRDS
33. BIRDS, BIRDBOOK, ACTORS

34. I KEPT MY DOCTOR
35. AN "I" - CHART
36. IT'S A RACE WAR
37. NEWS, IT'S A TOUCHDOWN
38. IT'S CASE BY CASE
39. IT'S NOBODY'S BUSINESS
40. BIRDS, COME FLY WITH ME
41. BIRDS, GEESE ON GRASS
42. BIRDS, EGGS IN ONE BASKET
43. A REAR STEAK
44. DEBUNKED
45. THE LATEST RAGE
46. LONELY AT THE TOP
47. A MAN SEVERING TIES
48. NEWS, CALL FOR SANCTIONS
49. BIRDS, ON THE FENCE
50. BIRDS, PATRIOT, NOT YET BEGUN
51. BIRDS, BIRD BOOK MOVIES
52. MEN OF STEAL
53. NEVER GETS OFF WRONG
54. NO-FLY ZONE
55. CONCLUSIONS?
56. NEWS, SUPPORT WOMEN
57. ONE-TON SOUP
58. PULLING STRINGS
59. PASSING SIGNS
60. NEWS, JERKS YES
61. BIRDS, DON'T LET CAT OUT
62. BIRDS, THE FLU SHOT
63. BIRDS, BOOK, F. NIGHTENGALE
64. NEWS, HAVE WOMAN'S BACK
65. NEWS, HAND IN HAND
66. PROOFS IN THE PUDDING
67. THE PROTESTEES
68. JOHN'S MARK

69. BIRDS, TAILGATING
70. BIRDS, GIVING THE BIRD
71. BIRDS, CANARY ISLANDS
72. NEWS, REACH THE STARS
73. ROLL CALL
74. ROYAL FLUSH
75. SKI PATROL
76. SILLY-CON-ALLEY
77. BIRDS, CANARY AND CAT
78. BIRDS, RYE BREAD, LOT'SA SEEDS
79. SINK YOUR TEETH
80. STOOL PIGEONS
81. NEWS, 2017 CONGRESS
82. NEWS, A SIDE OF THE AISLE
83. BIRDS, IT TAKES 2 WINGS
84. BIRDS, A DROP OVER
85. BIRDS, BOOK, LADYBIRD
86. NEWS, ALWAYS THINKING
87. KNEED TO PROTEST
88. NEWS, NO GOLDEN GRAB
89. THREE I CONS
90. TIE SCORE
91. NEWS, WALLA, DACA, CHAINA
92. NEWS, WHAT, WHERE, WHO
93. WATCHING HIS ASS
94. WATER UNDER THE BRIDGE
95. WE ARE VS. PROFILING
96. NEWS, WISHEE, WASHEE, WISH
97. WON BY A HARE
98. WORKING IN A CLIP JOINT
99. BIRDS, FOWL PLAY IS MISSING
100- BIRDS, MORE BIRDS?
101 THE BOOK TOP SHELF

1- NEWS, ADDRESSING CITIZENS CONCERNS

THIS IS A REMINDER THAT THERE WAS A SURPRISE TELEVISED EVENT FROM THE WHITEHOUSE IN JANUARY. A BIPARTISAN GROUP WAS TO FOCUS ON IMMIGRATION LAWS. THE PICTURE'S WORDS CONVEY THOUGHTS ABOUT THE OUTCOME OF THE MEETING.

1. NEWS, ADDRESSING CITIZENS CONCERNS

DO YOU HAVE ANY OPINIONS ABOUT THE CONTROVERSY CONCERNING IMMIGRATION IN AMERICA? TOONS WILL NOT OFFER ANY OPINIONS ON THIS ISSUE.

THERE IS MUCH INTEREST WITH THE TWO SIDES SHOOTING THEIR STUFF.

SOME SAY ALL OF US ARE IMMIGRANTS OR ARE HERE FROM PAST IMMIGRANTS. AMERICA IS KNOWN FOR ACCEPTING. THEY POINT TO THE STATUE OF LIBERTY AND GIVE ME YOUR TIRED AND POOR.

THE OTHER SIDE SAYS, WE DON'T NEED MORE TIRED OR POOR. THEY SAY ONLY PEOPLE THAT SHOW A PROBABILITY TO ASSIMILATE WELL IN THE U.S.A. SHOULD BE ACCEPTED HERE. THEY STRESS THE NEED TO BUILD THE WALL.

THIS IS P. C., -- POLITICALLY CONTROVERSIAL

WHAT DO YOU THINK?

2—NEWS, AND THE WINNER IS

AND THE WINNER IS

A CARTOON THAT MIGHT REMIND MANY TO REALIZE THEY COVERED THEIR EARS, EYES AND MOUTHS FOR MANY YEARS.

2—NEWS,   AND THE WINNER IS

WHERE DOES THE LINE STOP? SOME SAY THE DISCUSSION ABOUT THIS HARASSMENT SHOULD INCLUDE THE DRESS LINES. OTHERS SAY IT DOESN'T MATTER WHERE THE DRESS LINES ARE, THE LINE SHOULD NOT BE CROSSED.

THE TOPIC OF WHAT IS CONSENT OR REFUSAL IS DISCUSSED AT LENGTH IN LAW SCHOOLS.

THIS DISCUSSION HAS GONE ON AND ON.

TOONS THINKS THERE IS A FIRM ANSWER AND LOOKS FORWARD TO THE LEGAL COMMUNITY TO GET ITS HANDS AROUND THE ISSUE.

DO YOU HAVE A GRASP ON IT?

LOOK TO P. C., -- POTENTIALLY CONTROVERSIAL

3-- ANOTHER BALLBUSTER

ANOTHER BALLBUSTER

THE CARTOON IDEA IS FROM MY FRIEND'S BUSINESS CARD. HE WORKS FOR A BIG LEAGUE BAT COMPANY. IT PLAYS ON THE SLANG WORD FOR A PAIN IN THE BACKSIDE, A PAIN IN THE REAR, AN ANNOYING NUISANCE OR A BALLBREAKER.

3-- ANOTHER BALLBUSTER

DO YOU KNOW ANYONE THAT CONSTANTLY ANNOYS OTHERS? THEY COULD BE ANNOYING, OBNOXIOUS, EVEN TAUNTING AT TIMES. THEY QUESTION YOUR DECISIONS. WHY ARE YOU GOING TO A PLACE LIKE THAT, JUST PAY A LITTLE MORE, GO SOMEWHERE BETTER.

WHY BUY FURNITURE IN THAT PLACE, YOU'RE GONNA PAY MORE FOR LESS QUALITY.

WHY DON'T YOU WEAR A SHIRT THAT MATCHES?

THE WORST MAY BE, THE BALLBUSTER THAT ASKS ABOUT YOUR $$$ SITUATION, TELLING YOU HOW TO MAKE MORE $$$.

DO YOU ACCEPT THE BALLBUSTER INVASION OR DO YOU DISPLAY ANIMOSITY?

IT'S A P. C.,-- PILEDRIVER CLOUT

4- NEWS,   ANOTHER USE FOR SHOVELS

THE NEWSTOON POINTS OUT THAT THERE IS OPPOSITION TO THE BORDER WALL. THEY HAVE INTENTIONS TO GET RID OF IT IF THEIR PARTY HAS CONTROL IN THE NEXT ELECTION. THERE'S PROBABLY A NEED FOR SHOVELS IF YOU FOLLOW THIS GROUP.

4—NEWS,   ANOTHER USE FOR SHOVELS

WERE YOU EVER INVOLVED IN A CONSTRUCTION PROJECT USING BRICK AND MORTAR? WHEN THE PROFESSIONALS BUILD A WALL OR BARRIER, PLACING THE BRICKS OR BLOCKS LOOKS EASY. MOST INEXPERIENCED PEOPLE THAT TRY TO DO CONCRETE WORK GET TO UNDERSTAND THAT THERE ARE THOSE WHO CAN AND THOSE WHO CAN'T. GETTING THE CONCRETE BLOCKS AND CEMENT LEVEL IS AN ART. DO YOU THINK THAT POLITICIANS WHO TALK ABOUT SHOVEL READY JOBS WOULD BE GOOD WITH A SHOVEL? THEY DO TALK ABOUT SHOVEL READY JOBS. THERE ARE TIMES THAT POLITICIANS AND SHOVELS GO TOGETHER.

STRONG P. C.,-- PASSING CONCRETE

5-- AUTO BIOGRAPHIES

IT'S A MIDDLE SCHOOL LEVEL CARTOON. THE BIOGRAPHIES OF FAMOUS CARS AND FAMOUS PEOPLE ARE INTERESTING TO MANY, ESPECIALLY CAR ENTHUSIASTS. OVER THE YEARS, THE PRESIDENT'S CAR AND THE POPE MOBILE WERE DESCRIBED IN DETAIL, AS THE PROCESSION MOVED ALONG.

5-- AUTO BIOGRAPHIES

WHAT IS THE MOST EXPENSIVE CAR THAT YOU OCCUPIED ON A TRIP? THIS TOONOLOGIST'S FONDEST CAR MEMORY WAS IN THE BACK SEAT OF HIS UNCLE'S CAR. THE OLD CAR HAD A RUSTED OUT AREA ON THE FLOOR IN THE BACK, SO YOU COULD SEE THE ROAD THROUGH THE OPENING IN THE FLOOR.

THERE IS INTEREST IN CARS USED BY INFLUENTIAL PEOPLE. FOR HIS LAST VISIT TO AMERICA, THE POPE USED A FORD FOCUS, A 1984 RENAULT 4, AND A MIDSIZE FIAT 500L.

THE PRESIDENT RIDES IN A CADILLAC LIMO, FONDLY CALLED THE BEAST OR THE FIRST CAR OR CADILLAC ONE. YOU CAN REQUEST A TEST DRIVE AT YOUR TOP CHOICE DEALER. THEN YOU CAN CLAIM DRIVING THE BEST.

OF COURSE P. C., PRESERVING CARGO

BARE HUNTING SEASON

WHEN I HEARD THAT THERE WAS BEAR HUNTING IN NEW JERSEY, I FIGURED CHANGING TWO LETTERS AROUND CAN RESULT IN A CARTOON.
IN NEW JERSEY BEARS ARE HUNTED DURING DECEMBER. BEAR IS HUNTED IN SUSSEX, WARREN, PASSAIC AND OTHER COUNTIES. THE SEASON IN 2016 SHOWED A RECORD 607 BEARS TAKEN AND 3000 SINCE 2010.

6— BARE HUNTING SEASON

HAVE YOU EVER HUNG OUT IN AN NUDIST CAMP? WHICH IS MORE INTERESTING TO YOU, BEAR OR BARE HUNTING? IN THE CAMP, WHAT WOULD ATTRACT YOUR EYES THE MOST? YOU PROBABLY PRETEND TO BE UNCONCERNED WITH THE NUDITY OF THE OTHERS. IF THERE IS NO CONCERN, NON-DISTINGUISHING OPTICAL WEAR SHOULD BE ISSUED TO ALL.

MANY THINK THAT AMERICANS ARE TIMID FOR NOT ACCEPTING NUDITY AS IN OTHER COUNTRIES. MANY FEEL THAT NUDITY IS NATURAL AND SHOULD BE PERMITTED EVERYWHERE. IF THERE IS NO UNIFORM OR DRESS CODE FOR A JOB, NUDITY SHOULD BE FINE. WHEN A JURY IS PICKED, THE JUDGE STRESSES NO DISTRACTING INFLUENCES. NUDITY IN GOV'T AGENCIES WOULD BE A TEST FOR HARRASSMENT CONTROL AND MAKE VISIBLE ANYONE WEARING A SUICIDE VEST.

P.C. ---- PLENTY CONFUSION

BOARD DRY OR NO FLY

BOARD DRY OR NO FLY

SINCE THERE'S NO BOARDING PLANES WITH MORE THAN 3 OUNCES OF MOUTHWASH OR HAND SOAP, A CARTOON CAME TO ME. THIS CAN GIVE PEOPLE A HEADS UP OF WHAT'S TO COME. THEY MAY NOT ALLOW PEOPLE TO BOARD WITH MORE THAN 3 OUNCES IN THEIR BLADDER. A LIQUIDOMETER WILL DO THE MEASURING.

7--   BOARD DRY OR NO FLY

HAVE YOU EVER HAD AN ITEM REMOVED OR DISCARDED BEFORE BOARDING A PLANE? THE SECURITY PEOPLE CAN OPEN A STORE WITH THE THINGS THEY REMOVE FROM THE PASSENGERS.

THEY CAN PROBABLY OPEN TWO STORES WITH THE ITEMS NOT DETECTED AS WE ALL GO THROUGH THE MONITORING PROCEDURES.

ALTHOUGH THIS CARTOON IS JUST FOR SOME FUN, THERE IS A MACHINE USED BY UROLOGISTS THAT CAN GAUGE LIQUIDS REMAINING IN YOUR BLADDER.

IT MAY BE THAT EVERY AIRPORT SECURITY TEAM WILL INCLUDE A LIQUIDOLOGIST. AIRPORTS CAN HAVE A RADIOLOGY TEAM MEMBER CHECKING FOR WRONG STUFF CARRIED INTERNALLY. TOONS PREDICTS YOU WILL HAVE TO THINK TWICE ABOUT HAVING SOME BREWS BEFORE GOING ON A FLIGHT.

BOARD DRY OR NO FLY.   P.C.   PASSING CONTENTS

8—NEWS, BORDER CAPITALISM

WHEREVER THERE'S A FEW BUCKS TO BE MADE THERE WILL BE PARTICIPANTS. SO THE TOON SAYS THERE WILL BE PEOPLE TAKING ADVANTAGE OF ANY BUSINESS SPACE THAT IS NEAR THE BORDER WALL. WHO KNOWS WHAT BUSINESSES WILL WIND UP AT THE BORDER WALL.

NEWS, BORDER CAPITALISM

DO YOU HAVE SOME IDEAS FOR A BUSINESS AT THE BORDER WALL? TOONS SUGGESTS SLOT MACHINES ACCEPTING PESOS, TO HELP PAY FOR THE WALL.

THERE WILL BE PEOPLE VISITING THE WALL, SO FOOD AND MUSIC WOULD BE APPROPRIATE.

TAKE A PICTURE WITH A BRICKLAYER THAT BUILT THE WALL OR BUY A PICTURE OF THE WALL, OR ANY WALL SOUVENIR AND OBSERVE ITS FUTURE VALUE?

BY THE WAY, DON'T TAKE THE LADDERS, POGO STICKS OR HELICOPTER RIDES SERIOUS. THIS IS A CARTOON BOOK, WITH CARTOON COMMENTS.

THE WALL HAS BECOME A SERIOUS ISSUE. SOME WANT IT, SOME DON'T.

THE WALL MAY BE P. C., PURE CAPITALISM

9—BEEKEE AND BILHORN   TWEETERS

THE 2 BIRDS ARE DISCUSSING TWEETERS. THEY ARE DELIGHTED THAT SO MANY ARE NOW TWEETING. BH IS SAYING, THE 2 BIRDS SHOULD BE PROUD THAT THEY ARE THE ORIGINAL TWEETERS.

9--BEEKEE AND BILHORN, ORIGINAL TWEETERS

ARE YOU A BIG TIME TWEETER? IT'S AMAZING HOW THE WORLD HAS ERUPTED WITH THIS TWEETING CRAZE CONVEYING ALL KINDS OF THOUGHTS. FOR BEEKEE AND BILHORN THERE IS NO WORD LIMIT. THEY TWEET WHENEVER AND AS LONG AS THEY WISH. BIRDS ALL OVER THE WORLD TWEET. THE QUESTION IS, WHEN BIRDS OF A FAR EASTERN COUNTRY TWEET, DO THE NORTH AMERICAN BIRDS UNDERSTAND? DON'T YOU THINK THAT JUST LIKE PEOPLE, BIRDS TWEET IN DIFFERENT LANGUAGES?

THE CRANE IS THE NATIONAL BIRD OF CHINA. IT IS ALSO THE NATIONAL BIRD OF UGANDA AND SOUTH AFRICA. IF THE BIRDS WOULD BE ON THE SAME TREE, WOULD THEY UNDERSTAND EACH OTHER?

HERE IN AMERICA PEOPLE HAVE NO IDEA OF THE MEANING OF OTHERS' TWEETS. THE EAGLE IS AMERICA'S NATIONAL BIRD, ALSO THE BIRD OF GERMANY, MEXICO, INDONESIA, SERBIA AND ZAMBIA. ORNITHOLOGISTS MAY KNOW, BUT COMMON SENSE SAYS, JUST LIKE PEOPLE THEY DON'T KNOW WHAT EACH OTHER IS SAYING. IF THEY WANT PRIVACY, THEY TWEET SO ONLY THEY UNDERSTAND. LIKE PEOPLE THEY CHANGE TO A DIFFERENT LANGUAGE.

PAY ATTENTION, SEE IF TWEETING SOUNDS DIFFERENT WHEN YOU APPROACH BIRDS.

DO YOU THINK THE JAPANESE BIRD UNDERSTANDS A BIRD FROM INDIA?

10—BEEKEE AND BILHORN, NEW TAX PLAN

HERE THE 2 BIRDS ARE TAKING NOTE THAT THERE IS A NEW TAX PLAN. BH FEELS CONFIDENT THAT IT WILL HELP THEM TO HAVE A NICE NEST EGG.

10—BEEKEE AND BILHORN, NEW TAX PLAN

BK LOOKS TO BH FOR FINANCIAL ADVICE. BH KEEPS UP WITH WORLD EVENTS AND WORLD FINANCES. BK HEARS IT ALL BUT PAYS NO ATTENTION.

LIKE IN EVERYDAY HOMES THERE IS ONE WHO PAYS ATTENTION TO THE FINANCIAL SITUATION AND ONE THAT PAYS ATTENTION TO SPENDING, CAUSING A FINANCIAL SITUATION. BH AND BK PROBABLY HAVE MORE CONCERN OVER THEIR NEST EGGS THAN MANY OTHERS. BH IS MOST CONCERNED WITH FINANCE. THE TWO BIRDS ARE DEFINITELY INVESTED IN BILLS. THEIR MUTUAL FUNDS WOULD PROBABLY BE WITH FLEWDELITY OR FLUDENTIAL.

HOPEFULLY THE TOONOLOGIST DIDN'T LAY A BIG EGG WITH THE LAST TWO LINES.

IS YOUR NEST EGG FLYING HIGH?

11—BBEEKEE AND BILHORN, GIVE ME LIBERTY

THE 2 BIRDS NOT ONLY SHOW INTEREST IN BIRD SEED, BUT ALSO TOPICS PRESENT AND PAST. THE PATRICK HENRY HUMOR DISPLAYED IN THIS BIRDTOON MAKES B AND B MORE INTERESTING.

DO YOU REMEMBER THE PATRICK HENRY SPEECH?

11—BEEKEE AND BILHORN, GIVE ME LIBERTY

THE 2 BIRDS ARE INTO AMERICAN HISTORY. HERE BK AND BH ARE REMEMBERING THAT PATRICK HENRY WAS A DELEGATE TO THE SECOND VIRGINIA CONVENTION. HE WAS A KNOWN LAWYER AND ORATOR. HE IS EXTRA FAMOUS FOR HIS GIVE ME LIBERTY OR GIVE ME DEATH SPEECH, TAUGHT WHEN TAKING AMERICAN HISTORY. IT IS SAID THAT HE BECAME A LAWYER AFTER AN UNSUCCESSFUL ATTEMPT AT RUNNING A STORE. B AND B ARE HAPPY TO TELL US THAT HE DID BECOME THE GOVERNOR OF VIRGINIA. LOOK FORWARD TO MORE HISTORY FROM BH AND BK. DO YOU KNOW ANY PRESIDENT THAT FAILED WITH A BUSINESS BEFORE BECOMING PRESIDENT?

BORED OF EDUCATION

GOOD SPELLERS CAN FLING OUT PLENTY OF HOMONYMS. HERE USING WON, I MEAN ONE, A CARTOON IS SET UP. BORED IN PLACE OF BOARD OF EDUCATION IS QUITE APPROPRIATE.
DID YOU EVER PUT YOUR HEAD ON A DESK AND FALL FAST ASLEEP IN CLASS?

12— BORED OF EDUCATION

LET'S BE HONEST. THERE ARE CLASSROOMS WHERE A SLEEPING STUDENT IS THE ANSWER TO A TEACHER'S PRAYER. CERTAIN STUDENTS MAKE THE TEACHING ATMOSPHERE MORE PLEASANT WHEN SLEEPING, OR OUT WHEN REQUESTING THE BATHROOM. WHEN THERE'S A REQUEST FOR A BIG TIME MONITOR, THAT KID IS OFFERED.

IN ANOTHER SITUATION, WHEN THE TEACHER OR PROFESSOR FALLS ASLEEP AT THEIR DESK, THE MAJORITY OF STUDENTS DO NOT WANT A WAKE-UP CALL. LET'EM SLEEP WOULD BE WHISPERED BY ALL THE STUDENTS. THE ROOM WAS NEVER AS QUIET, AS MANY LEAVE GOING TO MORE FUN PLACES.

BORED OF EDUCATION CAN BE A TWO WAY STREET.

THE CLASS IS NOW, P. C., -- PROCEEDING CAUTIOUSLY

13— BUYING TIME

BUYING TIME

THIS NOT SO CREATIVE CARTOON CAN CREATE SOME SERIOUS DISCUSSIONS. BUYING TIME COVERS MANY ISSUES. USE OF A CREDIT CARD, THINKING TO PAY WHEN YOU GET THE $$$ CAN BE AN EXPENSIVE BUYING TIME PRICE. WHEN THE GOVERNMENT KICKS THE CAN DOWN THE ROAD, IT'S POLITICIANS BUYING TIME.

13— BUYING TIME

THINK OF ALL THE PEOPLE YOU KNOW WHO ARE POSTPONERS. IN ADDITION TO CREDIT CARD DEBT, HOW ABOUT THESE ISSUES: WILL START DIET SOON, STOP SMOKING MANANA & SAVE $$ FOR VACATION.

THE AVERAGE PERSON BUYING TIME USUALLY PAYS A PRICE, ESPECIALLY WITH CREDIT CARD INTEREST.

THE POLITICIAN WHO KICKS THE CAN DOWN THE ROAD STILL GETS PAID FOR A JOB NOT DONE.

IT IS TOON'S OPINION THAT YOU ARE PAYING FOR THE BROKEN CAN.

THERE ARE PEOPLE WHO GET ENGAGED JUST TO POSTPONE THE WEDDING AND PEOPLE THAT ALWAYS LOOK FOR A JOB NEXT WEEK.

HAVE YOU NOTICED THE NUMBER OF DIET PROGRAM ADVERTISEMENTS? COULD IT BE THAT THE ADS ARE AIMED AT THAT HERD OF PEOPLE WHO BUY TIME AND PROBABLY BUY SNACKS? IT'S P. C., -- PUSHING CANS

14— A CHANGE IN THE POLES

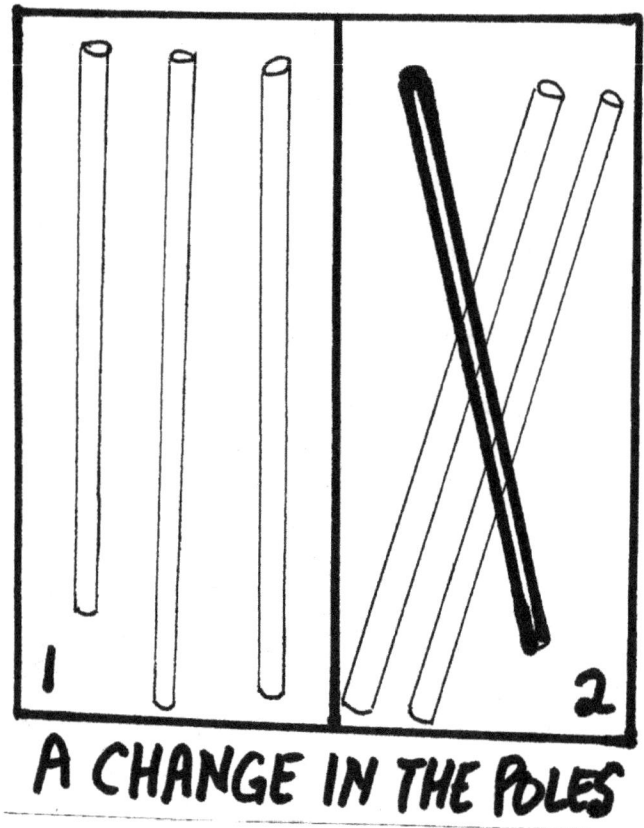

A CHANGE IN THE POLES

THIS CAN BE A NEWSTOON. T.V. QUOTES POLLS CONTINUOUSLY. THE NEWS PEOPLE POINT TO THE POLLS THAT SAY THE THINGS THEY LIKE BEST. THIS SIMPLE TOON IS A BEAUTY. THE CHANGE IN THESE POLES HAS NO MEANING, BUT SOMEONE WILL ATTEMPT AN EXPLANATION.

14— A CHANGE IN THE POLES

SINCE THE 2016 PRESIDENTIAL CAMPAIGN, POLLS HAVE BEEN A BIG PART OF THE NEWS. IT'S JUST ABOUT EVERYDAY THERE IS CONVERSATION ABOUT POLL NUMBERS RELATING TO THE MEDIA, TO THE CONGRESS AND THE PRESIDENT.

POLSTERS GET OPINIONS ON LIKEABILITY, DISLIKEABILITY, JOB ABILITY, TRUST, DISTRUST, BASICALLY ANYTHING THAT CAN BE SHOVED INTO THE NEWSCAST.

NINE MONTHS OR 3 YEARS BEFORE AN ELECTION POLLS ARE TAKEN. THEY POLL SENIORS, JUNIORS, FRESHMAN, TODDLERS, MAYBE BLACKS, WHITES AND COLOR BLIND.

THEY POLL ANYTHING, KNEELING, STANDING, SINGING, NOT KNOWING THE WORDS OR THE KEY.

LAST ELECTION, MOST GOT IT WRONG. LET'S HAVE BETTER USE OF POLES!! P. C., -- POLLS CHANGING

15— CITIES ADD SHOVEL READY JOBS

THIS IS A SAD, TROUBLING, CYNICAL AND CRITICAL PRESENTATION. THE POLITICIANS' USUAL OUTCRY IS, PROTECTING OUR CITIZENS IS NUMBER ONE.

DO YOU FEEL SAFE IN YOUR AREA?

15— CITIES ADD SHOVEL READY JOBS

THIS SCENE IS A REAL BLOTCH ON OUR SOCIETY. TOO MANY AREAS ARE KNOWN FOR CRIME, VIOLENCE AND UNREST. PEOPLE ARE UNCOMFORTABLE WITH THEIR CHILDREN ON THE STREETS OR IN A PARK. NEIGHBORHOOD TOUGHS TAKE $$ AND OTHER BELONGINGS FROM THOSE WHO ARE UNABLE TO PROTECT THEMSELVES. THE TOUGHS GET ROUGH WITH ELDERLY PEOPLE AS WELL AS THE YOUNG. THEY STEAL $$ AND EVEN GROCERIES. LATER IT BECOMES AN UPGRADE, WEAPONS AND BIGGER LOOT. IN MANY AREAS THE POLITICIANS ARE AGAINST STOP AND FRISK, EXCEPT IF IT MEANS ENTERING THE BUILDING THEY OCCUPY. EXISTING CRIME AND POOR SCHOOL ENVIRONMENT HELPS THEIR MEAL TICKET. MURDERS UP MEANS MORE MEETINGS AND MORE BLAME THROWN AROUND. USUALLY COMES A PITCH FOR MORE $$$ AND RE-ELECTION. THIS PICTURE IS TROUBLING WITH A CAPITAL 'T'. STOP THESE SHOVEL READY JOBS.

THERE NEEDS TO BE P. C.,   PREVENTING   CARNAGE

CRYING FOWL

A CARTOON LIKE WHAT APPEARED IN THE SCHOOL NEWSPAPER. THE HOMONYN GIVES THIS IDIOM A WHIMSICAL TOUCH, AS WELL AS ACTIVATING SOME THOUGHT. RECENTLY THERE'S BEEN A CONTINUOUS FLOW OF CRYING FOUL.

16— CRYING FOWL

IN 2017 THE BLAME AND COMPLAINING HAS COME FROM MANY DIRECTIONS. ONE GROUP IS ACCUSED OF NOT DEALING WITH THE FACTS, ONE GROUP IS UNHAPPY WITH THE FACTS, ONE GROUP DOESN'T BELIEVE THE FACTS, ONE GROUP DOESN'T WANT THE FACTS AND ONE GROUP FEELS THOSE ARE NOT THE FACTS.

ALL OF THESE GROUPS ARE CRYING FOUL. DURING 2017 THEY CRIED EVERYDAY. IN THIS COUNTRY THERE ARE GROUPS THAT ARE NOT CITIZENS OF THIS COUNTRY WHO CRY FOUL, ABOUT THIS COUNTRY.

THIS CARTOON STARTED OUT AS A SIMPLE LIGHTHEARTED IDEA BUT THE CRYING FOWL HAS GRAVITATED TO SOME SERIOUS SITUATIONS. MUCH OF THE CHIRPING IS FOUL.

THIS IS P. C., -- POLITICAL CRYING

ARE YOU CRYING?

17-- DENTISTS' WORK TIME

A WITTY, CARTOON FOR ELEMENTARY SCHOOL CHILDREN. AT LEAST THIS CARTOON IS NOT CONTROVERSIAL. MAYBE A LITTLE PAINFUL.

17-- DENTISTS' WORK TIME

DENTISTS, ENDODONTISTS, PERIODONTISTS, DENTAL SURGEONS DO TERRIFIC WORK HELPING OUR MOUTHS HAVE TEETH FOR OUR LATER YEARS. YEARS AGO, WHEN AGED PEOPLE OPENED THEIR MOUTHS IT COULD BE A SORROWFUL SIGHT.

IT WOULD BE NICE TO BE ABLE TO SAY THAT ALL PEOPLE CAN TAKE ADVANTAGE OF THE EXPERTISE PROVIDED BY THE DENTAL PROFESSION. BUT, NOT EVERYONE HAS ACCESS TO THE VARIOUS PROCEDURES THAT MAY BE NEEDED.

IN MY BOOK "GAMES OF SATISFACTION", I SAY WHEN A 6 YEAR OLD OPENS A MOUTH SHOWING MISSING TEETH IT'S CUTE. WHEN A SENIOR CITIZEN DOES THE SAME, NOT SO CUTE.

THE DENTIST IS P.C., PAIN CONTROL

18—NEWS, DOCTOR, DACA, VOTER?

THIS NEWSTOON SPOTLIGHTS THE CONFUSION THAT HAS DEVELOPED WITH BOTH SIDES OF THE ISSUE. THE TOON USES THE DACA SOUND TO ADD CONFUSION BY INSERTING DACA IN PLACE OF DOCTOR, IN THE I CAN KEEP MY DOCTOR FIASCO. SOME LOVE CONFUSION.

18—NEWS, DOCTOR, DACA, VOTER ?

LOOK AT THE PICTURE, THINK AS YOU WISH. THERE'S HEALTH CARE, ALIEN CHILDREN AND THE WALL IN SITE. THE QUESTIONS KEEP COMING.

WHY PAY A FINE FOR REFUSING HEALTH INSURANCE?

WAS KEEPING YOUR DOCTOR A LIE?

DO WE WANT A WALL?

WILL THE WALL KEEP OUT DRUGS?

WHO WILL WORK THE FARMS?

WHAT IS THE COST FOR THEIR LIVING HERE?

WHO PAYS THAT COST?

WHO CAN BECOME CITIZENS?

WHY DOESN'T CONGRESS SOLVE THE ISSUE?

A LITTLE NEWSTOON, DO YOU HAVE ANY QUESTIONS??

FLYING P. C.   POLITICAL CONFETTI

19--   A   DOG   POUND

THE TOONOLOGIST HOPES YOU PICKED UP ON THE MEANING OF A DOG POUND. IN THE PICTURE IT LOOKS MORE THAN A POUND.

19-- A DOG POUND

EVERYDAY THERE ARE DOGS BEING WALKED ON THE STREETS OF NEW YORK. SOME PEOPLE HANDLE MANY DOGS AT THE SAME TIME. DOGS LEAD WALKERS TO MAKE DEPOSITS AT FAVORITE DROPOFFS. MOST ARE EXCELLENT COMMUNITY MINDED CITIZENS. BUT THERE ARE SOME THAT DON'T TAKE THE RIGHT STEPS, WHICH RESULTS IN VERY UNHAPPY, UNSUSPECTING PEDESTRIANS MAKING THAT WRONG STEP. THERE ARE DOG WALKERS THAT CARRY THE SAME BAG FOR WEEKS, ALTERNATING THEIR DROPOFF PLACE ON DIFFERENT STREETS. THERE SHOULD BE SIGNS, PICK UP AFTER THE DOG DROPS OFF.

THERE MUST BE P. C., POOP CONTROL

WHAT DO YOU THINK THE PENALTY SHOULD BE FOR POOP LITTERING?

20—BEEKEE AND BILHORN,, NO BEAK TWEETS

BEEKEE AND BILHORN ARE JOKING ABOUT PEOPLE TWEETING WITHOUT HAVING BEAKS. HOW CAN THEY TWEET WITHOUT BEAKS? THEY ARE ASKING, FROM WHERE DO THESE PEOPLE TWEET? YOU COULD SAY THEY ARE KIDDING, SORT OF TONGUE IN BEAK.

20—BEEKEE AND BILHORN,   NO BEAK TWEETS

TWEETING IS NOW DISCUSSED DAILY ON TELEVISION NEWS PROGRAMS. OF COURSE, MOST OF THE TALK INVOLVES OUR COMMANDER-IN-TWEETS.

BK AND BH PAY COMPLETE ATTENTION TO CURRENT EVENTS. THEY OFTEN TWEET ABOUT HOW THEY WOULD VOTE. THEY HEAR THAT YOU MAY BE ABLE TO VOTE WITHOUT BEING A CITIZEN. JUST LIKE MANY CITIZENS, THE 2 BIRDS REALLY LOOK DOWN AT POLITICIANS.

B AND B THINK BIRDS SHOULD BE CITIZENS. THEY WOULD PETITION CONGRESS FOR LAWS AGAINST BIRD PREDATORS. THEY WOULD WANT LAWS TO SENTENCE BIRD KILLERS TO LIFE IN A CAGE WITHOUT PAROLE.

21—BEEKEE AND BILHORN,,   DON'T SHOOT

NOT EVEN THE START OF THIS HISTORICAL QUOTE IS CORRECT. DON'T FIRE TILL YOU SEE THE WHITES OF THEIR EYES, WAS UTTERED AT THE BATTLE OF BUNKER HILL. THE 2 BIRDS LIKE TO PUT SOME BIRD STUFF INTO HISTORICAL EVENTS.

21—BEEKEE AND BILHORN,   DON'T SHOOT

THE DISCUSSION FOCUSED ON WAS IT THE GENERAL OR THE COLONEL WHO CALLED OUT, DON'T FIRE TILL YOU SEE THE WHITES OF THEIR EYES. THE STORY IS THAT GUN POWDER WAS SCARCE. AS THE OFFICERS SAW THE SHORT SUPPLY, THEY CAUTIONED THE SOLDIERS ONLY PULL THE TRIGGER WITH A CONFIDENT HIT.

SOME SAY IT WAS GENERAL WM. PRESCOTT, OTHERS SAY IT WAS COLONEL ISRAEL PUTNAM. BEEKEE JOKED IF THE COLONEL WAS A FULL BIRD, IT WAS THE COLONEL, THAT SAID IT.

THE 2 BIRDS AGREE THAT BOTH SHOULD GET THE CREDIT. IF BK AND BH GAVE THE ORDERS, IT WOULD BE DON'T DROP ANY UNTIL YOU ARE RIGHT ABOVE THE HEADS.

22—BEEKEE AND BILHORN,, BLUEBIRD THE PIRATE

THIS BIRDTOON LISTS SOME OF THE CHARACTERS IN BilHorn's BIRD BOOK. SO PROUD OF FAMOUS BIRDS, EVERYTHING IN THE BOOK WILL BE COMPLIMENTARY TO THEM. IN THE BilHorn BOOK THERE WILL BE A HERO BLUEBIRD THE PIRATE.

22—BEEKEE AND BILHORN, BLUEBIRD THE PIRATE

IN BILHORN'S BIRD BOOK EVERY CHARACTER CAN FLY. ROBINHOOD WILL HAVE A FLOCK OF MERRY BIRDS, HAVING DIFFERENT METHODS TO TAKE CARE OF BUSINESS, DOING GOOD FOR ALL.

BIGBIRD WILL BE SO LARGE THAT THERE WILL BE NO ASSISTANCE NEEDED. BIGBIRD'S WING SPAN WILL BE ABLE TO ENCLOSE ANY ADVERSARY THAT 'S LOOKING TO DO EVIL.

BLUEBIRD THE PIRATE WILL HAVE A COLONY TO HELP FIGHTING FOR JUSTICE.

IN COMIC BOOKS SUPER HEROES ARE MADE TO FLY. IN BILHORN'S BOOK THERE ARE BIRDS, OF COURSE THEY CAN FLY. THE ADVERSARIES WILL BE CONFRONTED BY THE FLOCK OF FLYING CHARACTERS.

THEY WILL ALL COMMUNICATE BY TWEETING. THEY WILL REPORT TO THE COMMANDER-IN-TWEET.

23—NEWS, DOING THE CAN-CAN

THIS NEWSTOON SHOWS A COUPLE OF GUYS DOING THE CAN-CAN BECAUSE THEY THINK THEY CAN. IT'S HARD TO BELIEVE THAT A SENATOR OR A CONGRESSMAN THAT OFTEN KICKS THE CAN DOWN THE ROAD, ALSO TAKES THE LIBERTY OF TAPPING A CAN DOWN THE ROAD.

23—NEWS, DOING THE CAN-CAN

TO MANY, THIS NEWSTOON IMAGE IS PROBABLY THOUGHT OF AS COARSE, HARSH AND TROUBLING.

THE ACTION WOULD BE THOUGHT OF AS NERVY AND CONTEMPTUOUS.

THOSE WHO PUBLICLY BELIEVE THIS DID HAPPEN, EVALUATE IT AS TWISTED AND BACKHANDED.

DO YOU THINK SUCH ELITE MEMBERS OF SOCIETY WOULD DO THIS KIND OF CAN-CAN?

HOW NAÏVE DO YOU WANT TO BE? AREN'T THESE GUYS AWAY FROM HOME HALF THE YEAR? ARE THEY HOUSED IN A MONASTERY OR ARE THERE MANY SOCIAL FUNCTIONS FOR THEM TO ATTEND?

DO YOU EVER SEE THEM UNSHAVEN AND SCUFFY LOOKING? MAYBE THEY SHOULD END KICKING AND TAPPING ALL CANS.

UNACCEPTABLE P. C., -- POSITIVELY CONTEMPTUOUS

FINAL SAIL

A SIMPLE CARTOON WITH SAIL IN PLACE OF THE USUAL SALE IN FINAL SALE SIGNS. THIS PICTURE IS SUPPOSED TO SHOW A MUTILATED SAIL, NOT TO SAIL AGAIN. IT'S A HOMONYM THAT SHOULD SAIL.

24-- FINAL SAIL

IN 2017 THERE WERE 2 WOMEN AND THEIR DOGS RESCUED AFTER DRIFTING HUNDREDS OF MILES FOR 5 MONTHS. THE MOTOR FAILED, THE SAILS DID NOT KEEP THEM ON COURSE, IT WAS ALMOST THEIR FINAL SAIL. THE USUAL FINAL SALE SIGNS APPEAR IN STORES TO ATTRACT CUSTOMERS. THOSE SAME SIGNS COULD BE IN THOSE SAME STORES FOR YEARS. WHAT IT MEANS IS, THESE FINAL SALE SIGNS ARE DISPLAYED UNTIL THERE'S A REAL FINAL SALE. THE SIGNS SHOULD READ, THESE ARE THE FINAL, FINAL SALE SIGNS. THERE WILL BE NO OTHER SALE SIGNS AFTER THESE SIGNS. THESE ARE FINAL SALE SIGNS MADE TO LAST. THIS WRITING IS UNCLEAR, WHAT SHOULD BE CLEAR IS THAT THE STORE IS NOT CLOSING. THOSE STORES THAT HAVE FINAL SALE SIGNS AND ARE STILL OPEN YEARS LATER WITH THE SAME FINAL SALE SIGNS DISPLAYED, TRICK ME ALL THE TIME. WHEN I SEE THE (P. C.) PRETEND CLEARANCE SIGN, I'M LOOKING.

GETTING A LEG UP

THIS UPBEAT CARTOON CAN CONJURE UP VARIOUS THOUGHTS AND MEMORIES. TOONS WILL TAKE A DIFFERENT POSITION ABOUT CHEERLEADERS AND THE SOCIAL ASPECTS ATTACHED TO THEM.

25-- GETTING A LEG UP

IT'S BELIEVED THAT SCHOOL CHEERLEADING SQUADS CONSIST OF THE PRETTIEST, MOST POPULAR GIRLS IN THE SCHOOL. TOONS IS SUGGESTING A DIFFERENT VIEWPOINT. HOW ABOUT SOME EQUALITY OR MAYBE CALL IT INEQUALITY ON THE SQUAD.

THE SQUAD OF 12, SHOULD CONSIST OF 4 PRETTY, CUTELY SHAPED AGILE GIRLS. BUT ALSO, THE SQUAD SHOULD INCLUDE 4 SHORT ROTUND STUDENTS WHOSE LEGS WOULD NOT RAISE MUCH ABOVE THE KNEE. THEY WOULD WEAR THE USUAL SQUAD UNIFORM. ANOTHER 4 COULD BE ANY SIZE, REFUSING TO WEAR A UNIFORM OR PERFORM ANY COREOGRAPHED STEPS.

HOW ABOUT INCLUDE ALL KINDS? DON'T YOU THINK EQUALITY IS IMPORTANT? DON'T BE A HYPOCRITE. COULD BE P. C., --- POLITE CONCERN

26-- GETTING RID OF L D Ls

THIS CARTOON SPOOFS THE DOCTOR'S ADVICE AND DIRECTION TO PATIENTS THAT HAVE A CHOLESTEROL PROBLEM. IF LDLs ARE TOO HIGH, GET RID OF LDLs.

26— GETTING RID OF LDLs

CROSSING OUT THE LETTERS WILL NOT LOWER THE RISK FOR GETTING CLOGGED ARTERIES.

IT WOULD BE NICE FOR IT TO BE THIS SIMPLE.

THIS TOON GUY HAS HAD BAD TIMES BECAUSE OF CLOGGED ARTERIES.

TOONS ADVISES GOOD DIET, ENOUGH EXERCISE AND HAVING FUN PLAYING WITH CHILDREN.

WHEN PEOPLE ASK YOU, HOW ARE YOU DOING, DO YOU OFFER ANY MEDICAL NUMBERS?

PEOPLE CAN RELEASE EYE PRESSURE, BLOOD PRESSURE, A1C EVEN LDLs, BUT PEOPLE USUALLY JUST SAY O.K. OR FINE OR HANGIN IN. THERE ARE SOME THAT WILL BOMBARD YOU WITH THEIR AILMENTS FROM HEAD TO TOE, THEN TELL YOU ABOUT OTHERS.

THERE'S NEED TO BE P. C.,   PREVENT CLOGGING HOW ARE YOUR LDLs?

27—NEWS, GREAT WALL OF CHAINA

GREAT WALL OF CHAINA

THE NEWSTOON IS EXPRESSING THE POSSIBILITY THAT A BORDER WALL WILL BE BUILT. THE POLES ARE UP IN THE AIR. ACTUALLY THE TITLE REFERS TO THE CHAIN MIGRATION ISSUE. THE QUESTION ASKS, SHOULD NON-CITIZENS HAVE AN OPTION TO BRING RELATIVES TO AMERICA? OR WILL THERE BE A WALL?

27—NEWS, GREAT WALL OF CHAINA

THE WALL REPRESENTS THOSE WHO ARE LOOKING TO FORBID CHAIN IMMIGRATION. FOR THIS, CONGRESS MUST ENACT LAWS AND FUND THE WALL. THE SAME THOUGHT WANTS TO END THE LOTTERY SYSTEM OF IMMIGRATION.

IT IS THE JOB OF CONGRESS TO SET THE LAWS THAT DECIDE WHO, HOW, AND WHEN PEOPLE CAN BE ADMITTED INTO THIS COUNTRY.

IF THEY CAN'T FIGURE OUT AN ACCEPTABLE SYSTEM, MAYBE, THERE SHOULD BE A WALL PREVENTING CONGRESS ENTERING THEIR OFFICE BUILDING.

THE TOONOLOGIST LIKED THE IDEA OF THE "GREAT WALL OF CHAINA" FOR THE CARTOON TITLE. FOR CONGRESS IT COULD BE THE STONEWALL OF CONGRESS.

THIS IS NOW IT'S P. C., PITIFUL CONGRESS

28— HE BED VETS

HE BED VETS

THEY ARE ALL TALKING ABOUT WHOM THE GOVERNMENT WILL VET. THEY CAN'T VET'EM FROM THAT COUNTRY, THEY DIDN'T VET THEM ENOUGH FROM THE OTHER PLACE. HERE'S A GUY WHO DOES VET.

28— HE BED VETS

THEY SAY, IT'S IMPORTANT TO BE ABLE TO VET ENTERING IMMIGRANTS.

THEY ALSO VET JUDGES AND PROSPECTIVE CABINET MEMBERS. THIS MEANS QUESTIONING AND INVESTIGATING BACKGROUNDS. SO THE CUSTOMER IN THE BED AND MATTRESS STORE, ASKING THE SALESMAN AN UNEASY NUMBER OF QUESTIONS IS VETTING THE BED.

THERE ARE MANY QUESTIONS THAT SHOULD BE ASKED WHEN BUYING A MATTRESS. YOU USUALLY SPEND ONE-THIRD OF EVERYDAY ON THE MATTRESS.

THERE SHOULD BE NOBODY UPSET THINKING THERE'S A POKE AT A DIALECT HERE. JUST USING A WORD THAT CAN RESULT IN SOME HUMOR.

THIS BOOK LIKES P.C., -- PEACEFULLY COMFORTABLE .

HOME SCHOOLING

HOME SCHOOLING

ALTHOUGH DISCIPLINE IS SUPPOSED TO BE TAUGHT IN THE HOME, THIS METHOD IS FROWNED UPON. THE PADDLE LABELED BOARD 4 EDUCATION IS A TRY TO GET A SMILE (NOT FROM THE KID).

29— HOME SCHOOLING

THERE ARE MANY ADVERTISEMENTS FOR HOME SCHOOLING. IT SEEMS LIKE THERE ARE ENOUGH PEOPLE DISSATISFIED WITH PUBLIC SCHOOLS, PUTTING THE HOME SCHOOLING SERVICE IN PLAY. MAYBE PEOPLE WANT SCHOOLS TO FOCUS ON ACADEMICS RATHER THAN THE TURN TO A SOCIAL ATMOSPHERE. THE FUNNY HAT DAY, PAJAMA DAY, OPPOSITE DAY, PIZZA PARTY DAY, VALENTINES DAY AND OTHER SOCIAL CREATIONS HAVE REPLACED TOO MUCH OF THE 3Rs CLASS TIME.

THERE'S MUCH TO BE SAID FOR SOCIAL ACTIVITIES, BUT NOT EVERYONE AGREES TO HOW IT'S BEING BALANCED.

ONE MIGHT SAY, IT SHOULD ONLY BE THE 3Rs PLUS THE 3Cs, COMPUTERS, CIVICS, CITIZENSHIP. THE Cs SHOULD NOT FEATURE CUPCAKES.

SCHOOLS ARE P. C., PRESENTING CUPCAKES

30-- A HORSE DRAWN WAGON

A WHIMSICAL CARTOON, APPROPRIATE FOR SCHOOL AGE KIDS. IT'S A HORSE USING A MARKER, TO DRAW THE WAGON. SO, A HORSE DRAWN WAGON.

30-- A HORSE DRAWN WAGON

THIS COULD BE A NEWSTOON. THIS ONE WOULD BE FROM NEW YORK CITY WHEN THERE WAS A PUSH TO ELIMINATE THE HORSE AND CARRIAGE INDUSTRY FROM AROUND CENTRAL PARK.

THE HORSES AND CARRIAGES ARE LINED UP ON THE STREETS ALONG THE PARK WAITING FOR PASSENGERS. TOURISTS, ROMANTICS AND SOME LOOKING FOR A RELAXING RIDE GOING THOUGH THE PARK, ENJOYING THE BEAUTIFUL SCENERY.

PEOPLE ARE CONSTANTLY TAKING PHOTOGRAPHS OF, AND WITH THE HORSES AND CARRIAGES AS THEY ARE WAITING FOR PASSENGERS.

IT ADDS TO THE TOURIST INDUSTRY AND ALSO THE SHOVEL BUSINESS.

GET THE DRIFT?

IT'S P. C., --- PERMITTING CARRIAGES

31—BEEKEE AND BILHORN, FAMOUS PEOPLE TWEET

BEEKEE AND BILHORN ENJOY CONVERSATING ABOUT THE TWEETING DONE BY FAMOUS PEOPLE. THEY LIKE DISCUSSING IDEAS OF THEIR COMMANDER-IN-TWEET.

31—BEEKEE AND BILHORN, FAMOUS PEOPLE TWEET

THE COMMANDER-IN-TWEET IS THE MOST FAMOUS TWEETER ENJOYED BY THE 2 BIRDS. THERE ARE TWEETS ABOUT INFORMATION LOST, INFORMATION DETROYED, INFORMATION IN UNSECURE PLACES AND TWEETS THAT CAN CAUSE PEOPLE TROUBLE.

THERE ARE TWEETS COVERING THE WALL AND BORDER SECURITY.

THERE ARE TWEETS ABOUT THE HIGH RISE IN THE STOCK MARKET.

IF YOU NOTICE THIS BOOK CONTAINS NEWSTOONS ON ALL ISSUES.

BK AND BH LIKE TO STAY NEUTRAL AS THEY OVER HEAR ALL THE TWEETED VIEWPOINTS.

IF YOU ARE THINKING THAT THE 2 BIRDS HAVE MUCH INFORMATION BECAUSE OF THEIR BIRDS EYE VIEW, IT'S THINKING FOR THE BIRDS, BUT IN A GOOD WAY.

32—BEEKEE, AND BILHORN, KILLING BIRDS

THIS BIRDTOON SHOWS ONE OF THOSE BIRD IDIOMS THAT IS UPSETTING TO BEEKEE AND BILHORN.

32—BEEKEE, AND BILHORN, KILLING BIRDS

IN BOOKS AND EVERYDAY CONVERSATION BIRDS ARE REFERENCED.

MOST BIRD REFERENCES MAKE BK AND BH HAPPY, BUT SOME ARE VERY ANNOYING FOR THEM. A FEW BIRD SAYINGS THAT THE 2 BIRDS DISLIKE ARE, IT'S STRICTLY FOR THE BIRDS, THE PERSON IS A BIRDBRAIN AND EVEN, HE'S JUST A FLY BY NIGHT. THEY DEFINITELY DO NOT ENJOY HEARING, LOOKING LIKE THE CAT THAT SWALLOWED THE CANARY, WHICH MEANS THEY MIGHT HAVE LOST A FRIEND. BEEKEE AND BILHORN LIKE TO DEBATE THE BIRD BRAIN ISSUE. THEY POINT TO THE PART PLAYED BY HOMING PIGEONS CARRYING STRATEGIC MESSAGES DURING WARTIME.

B AND B KNOW MANY BIRDS MIGRATE TO WARMER CLIMATES FOR BETTER SURVIVAL CONDITIONS. THEY KNEW TO DO THIS BEFORE THE HUMAN SNOWBIRDS.

33—BEEKEE AND BILHORN,   ACTORS

BILHORN'S BIRD BOOK WILL INCLUDE FAMOUS ACTORS WITH BIRD NAMES. ALL OF THESE ACTORS WILL BE IN A GROUP THAT WATCH AND LOOKOUT FOR THE SAFETY OF BIRDS. THEY WILL PROUDLY BE CALLED ORNI-ACTORVISTS.

33—BEEKEE AND BILHORN, ACTORS

JUST TO NOTE, THERE ARE MANY MOVIES THAT FEATURE OR INCLUDE BIRDS. THEIR ROLES ARE VARIED FROM FRIGHTENING TO BEING FRIENDLY. ISN'T THERE PIGEON PRESENCE IN SEA OF LOVE, FORREST GUMP AND MOONRAKER?

IN BILHORN'S BIRD BOOK, THE ORNI-ACTORVISTS WILL LIVE IN THE TOWN BIRD-IN-HAND, OCCUPYING BUILDINGS BUILT LIKE DOME SHAPED AVIARIES. THE ORNI-ACTORVISTS WILL FILM DOCUMENTARIES PROMOTING SAFETY AND EDUCATION ABOUT BIRDS. BILHORN'S BOOK WILL INCLUDE A LIST OF INTERESTING BOOKS ABOUT BIRDS. THERE WILL BE BOOKS TO IDENTIFY BIRDS, BOOKS FOR CHOOSING BIRD PETS, BOOKS ABOUT MIGRATION, ECOLOGY, MOST COLORFUL EVEN ABOUT SEABIRDS AND SONGBIRDS.

34— I KEPT MY DOCTOR

I KEPT MY DOCTOR

THAT NEW INSURANCE LAW RESULTING IN MANY NOT ABLE TO KEEP THEIR DOCTOR WAS AVOIDED BY THIS PATIENT. SHE MARRIED HER DOCTOR.

34—   I KEPT MY DOCTOR

WITHOUT TAKING A STAND RELATING TO THE TRUTH ABOUT BEING ABLE TO KEEP YOUR DOCTOR WITH THE NEW HEALTH CARE LAW, THIS CARTOON SHOWS THERE'S MORE WAYS TO ACCOMPLISH A GOAL.

HERE SHE KEEPS HER DOCTOR AND TAKES HIM HOME. THE CARTOON IS SUPPOSED TO BE WITTY, BUT THE KEEPING YOUR DOCTOR ISSUE WINDS UP FAR FROM FUNNY.

TOONS BELIEVES THAT THE MEDICAL PROFESSIONALS HAVE THE BEST INTENTIONS FOR THE PATIENTS. BUT IT SEEMS THE ADMINISTRATORS ARE ONLY IN IT AS A BUSINESS. THE INSURANCE RULES MAY MAKE IT DIFFICULT TO KEEP YOUR DOCTOR WHEN BUSINESS COMES BEFORE PATIENT SYMPATHY.

 PATIENTS SHOULD BE TREATED LIKE RELATIVES. MARRYING YOUR DOCTOR SHOULD GIVE YOU GOOD HEALTH CARE. THIS IS P. C. , -- PATIENT CARE

AN I-CHART

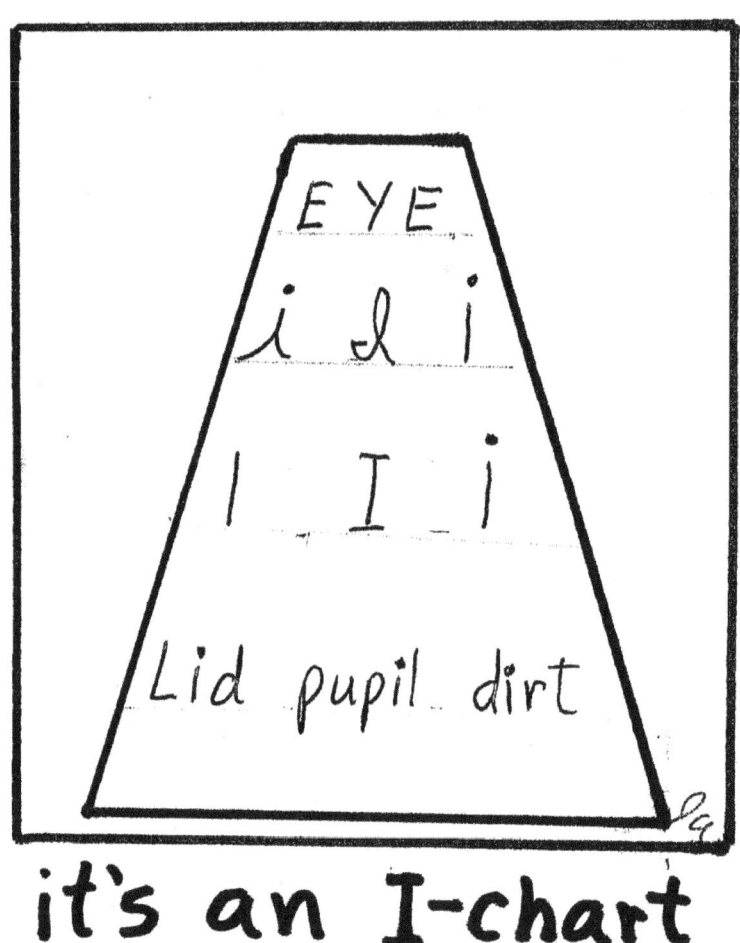

JUST A THOUGHT THAT AN EYE CHART SHOULD CONTAIN MANY IZE (I, I, I, i), THEN IT CAN REALLY BE CALLED AN I-CHART.

35-- AN I-CHART

THE EYE CHART HAS RECOMMENDED EYEGLASSES TO MILLIONS. THANK GOODNESS FOR EYEGLASSES THAT ASSIST SEEING THE FINER LETTERS FROM THAT CHAIR ABOUT 20 FEET AWAY FROM THE CHART.

WAS IT SALVINO D'ARMATE WHO INVENTED THEM IN 1285? EYE GLASSES WERE FIRST MADE TO CORRECT FAR SIGHTEDNESS. THE LENS WAS MADE OF QUARTZ AND THE FRAMES WERE BONE OR METAL. THE WORD LENS COMES FROM ITS SIMILAR SHAPE TO THE LENTIL BEAN.

IN 1727, THE FRAMES WENT OVER THE EARS AND NOSE, CREATED BY EDWARD SCARLETT OF BRITAIN. BEN FRANKLIN IS CREDITED WITH INVENTING BIFOCALS.

                              PATIENT TRIES P. C., PEEKY CHARTY

IT'S A RACE WAR

THIS CARTOON HAS TO BE THE WORST IN THE BOOK. WHEN LOOKING AT IT, YOU ASK WHAT'S IT ABOUT? THERE'S NO STORY, NOTHING FUNNY OR INTERESTING. THERE MUST HAVE BEEN AN ORIGINAL PURPOSE, BUT RIGHT NOW IT IS ELUDING THE TOONOLOGIST.
DO YOU SEE ANYTHING IN THIS TOON?

36-- IT'S A RACE WAR

TWO WORDS APPEAR TOGETHER AND A CARTOON THOUGHT EVOLVES. DOG POUND, HORSE DRAWN, CRYING FOUL, EYE CHART OR RACE WAR.

THE TOONOLOGIST HOPES SOME HUMOR OR THOUGHT COMES FROM THE CARTOON.

HERE A CARTOON WAS DRAWN, BUT DID HUMOR BURST OUT WITH THE IDEA OF A WAR DURING A RACE?

THIS CARTOON IS A RIDICULUOS, REPULSIVE, DISTASTEFUL FARCE.

MAYBE THERE WAS TO BE MORE TO IT.

MAYBE THE NO WINNERS SIGN RECUES THE CARTOON? DO YOU SEE ANYTHING MEANINGFUL?

THIS SHOWS THAT NOT ALL CARTOONS MAKE SENSE.

IT IS P.C., --- PERFECTLY CONFUSING.

37—NEWS, IT'S A TOUCHDOWN

IT'S A TOUCHDOWN

HERE THEY ARE AT IT AGAIN. THE NEWS WAS FLOODED WITH UNSAVORY POLITICIANS AND THEIR ACTIONS AGAINST WOMEN. THE AMOUNT OF MEDIA COVERAGE INSPIRED THIS BOOK TO INCLUDE MANY NEWSTOONS TOUCHING ON THAT ISSUE.

37—NEWS,   IT'S A TOUCHDOWN

RECENTLY A NUMBER OF SENATORS WERE INTERVIEWED ON RADIO. THEY SEEM TO AGREE THAT THE SENATE HAS BEEN DYSFUNCTIONAL. THEY DIDN'T GET A NEW APPROPRIATIONS BILL FOR FUNDING THE MILITARY.

IT WAS SAID THAT THE BIGGEST ENEMY OF OUR MILITARY WAS THE CONGRESS.

TOONS, DOES HAVE THE BACKS OF THE CONGRESS.

IF ONE LOOKS AT THE CARTOON, SOME MAY THINK THESE CONGRESSMEN ARE FUNCTIONING.

ACTUALLY, THERE IS AN ABSENCE OF HUMOR HERE.

FOR MANY REASONS, THERE IS A LOW OPINION OF CONGRESS. TOO MUCH BICKERING, NOT ENOUGH ACCOMPLISHED FOR THE PEOPLE.

THIS UNCOMFORTABLE P. C., POMPOUS CONTACT

38— IT'S CASE BY CASE

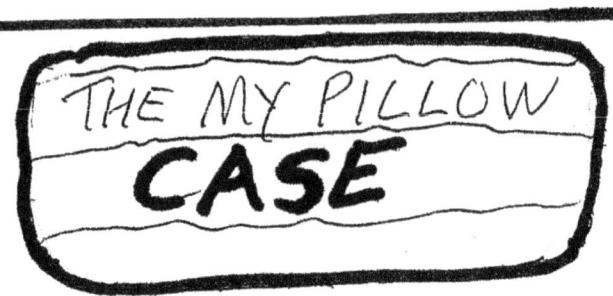

PUTTING TOGETHER TELEVISION ADVERTISEMENTS AND DETECTIVE PROGRAMS EQUALS THE CARTOON, THE MY PILLOW CASE.

38-- IT'S CASE BY CASE

THE WRITINGS ON THE TOON HAVE DOUBLE MEANINGS.

FOR BEST UNDERSTANDING, THERE'S A NEED FOR SOME ANALYSIS.

WHO TOOK THE MY PILLOW CASE CAN MEAN WHO ABSCONDED WITH IT, OR WHO IS THE DETECTIVE THAT HAS BEEN ASSIGNED TO THE CASE?

WHAT ARE THE THINGS THAT THE DETECTIVE IS DOING ABOUT MY PILLOW CASE?

IS THIS PILLOW CASE BEING HANDLED CAREFULLY?

EACH SENTENCE HAS BEEN WELL THOUGHTOUT.

THIS IS ONE OF THE TOONOLOGIST'S FAVORITE.

DO YOU THINK YOU CAN GET YOUR HEAD ON OR INTO THE MY PILLOW CASE?

OF COURSE IT'S P.C.,   PILLOW CASE.

IT'S NOBODY'S BUSINESS

IT'S NOBODY'S BUSINESS

PUTTING TOGETHER THE LARGE NUMBER OF STORES THAT ARE VACANT WITH THE OFTEN USED IT'S NOBODY'S BUSINESS, THIS CARTOON IS FOR RENT.

39—   IT'S NOBODY'S BUSINESS

WHEN AREA STORES CLOSE DOWN. PEOPLE ASK, WHY DID THEY CLOSE?

PEOPLE UTTER THE OBVIOUS SET OF ANSWERS;

THE RENT WAS INCREASED.

THEY WEREN'T MAKING ANY $$$.

THE BUSINESS PUT A STRAIN ON THE FAMILY.

WHO WANTS TO WORK THOSE LONG HOURS?

THERE'S MUCH TOO MUCH COMPETITION.

I THINK IT WAS HEALTH ISSUES.

SOME OFFER NASTY OPINIONS LIKE THEY REALLY DIDN'T KNOW HOW TO RUN A BUSINESS OR ONE OF THEM WAS PROBABLY STEALING.

YOU MIGHT GET THE BEST ANSWER FROM THIS CARTOON, IT'S NOBODY'S BUSINESS.

IF YOU NEED P. C.,   PERSONAL CONCERN

40—BEEKEE AND BILHORN, COME FLY WITH ME

BILHORN ENJOYS WHEN BEEKEE SINGS. THERE ARE DAYS WHEN THE SINGING LASTS FOR HOURS.

40—BEEKEE AND BILHORN, COME FLY WITH ME

THERE ARE PLENTY OF SONGS ABOUT BIRDS AND HAVING BIRDS IN THE TITLE.

BK KNOWS MOST OF THEM. HERE IS A SMALL LIST.

AND YOUR BIRD CAN SING

HIGH FLYING BIRD

HUMMINGBIRD

MOCKINGBIRD HILL

YELLOWBIRD

TINY SPARROW

BLUEBIRD

BYE, BYE BLACKBIRD

THERE ARE BIRD SONG RECORDINGS, BY THE BEATLES, PETER, PAUL AND MARY, NEIL YOUNG, CARLY SIMON, JAMES TAYLOR, SEALS AND CROFT AND MANY MORE GREAT ARTISTS.

BEEKEE TRIES TO TWEET THE TUNES, BUT CANNOT DO MUCH WITH THE WORDS.

41—BEEKEE AND BILHORN, GEESE ON GRASS

BK AND BH ARE VERY OBSERVANT AS THEY FLY OVER THE PARKS. EVERY ONCE IN A WHILE THERE'S A GAGGLE FERTILIZING THE GRASS.
THE 2 BIRDS ARE CONCERNED ABOUT THE KIDS STEPPING INTO THAT FERTILIZER.

41—BEEKEE AND BILHORN,   GEESE ON GRASS

B AND B ARE IMPRESSED WHEN THE GEESE FLY IN THEIR "V" FORMATION. THE FLYING GEESE IS CALLED A SKEIN. BILHORN LETS OTHERS KNOW THERE'S A REASON THAT THE BIRDS FLY IN THE "V" FORMATION. THE LEAD FLYER STAYS IN THE LEAD UNTIL TIRING, AT WHICH TIME THERE IS A REPLACEMENT.

EACH BIRD FLIES, A LITTLE ABOVE THE BIRD IN FRONT OF IT, GETTING LESS WIND RESISTANCE. THE LEAST WIND POSITIONS ARE FOR THE MOST TIRED BIRDS. THEY TAKE TURNS IN THE DIFFERENT POSITIONS OF THE "V" FORMATION.

COULD YOU THINK OF ANOTHER REASON THAT THE BIRDS WOULD RATHER BE ABOVE THE ONE IN FRONT OF IT, INSTEAD OF BELOW?

42—BEEKEE AND BILHORN, EGGS IN ONE BASKET

BILHORN REACTS TO SAYINGS THAT MIGHT RELATE TO BIRDS. BH LIKES IT'S A FEATHER IN YOUR CAP AND YOU'RE A SHARP OLD BIRD.

42—BEEKEE AND BILHORN,   EGGS IN ONE BASKET

ALTHOUGH THE 2 BIRDS KNOW MOST OF THE BIRD PROVERBS, IDIOMS AND SUCH, THEY FEEL THAT MOST HAVE NOTHING TO DO WITH THEM.

SOME EXAMPLES ARE, A WISE OLD OWL, PROUD AS A PEACOCK, THE GOOSE THAT LAID THE GOLDEN EGG, HAVING AN EAGLE EYE, THE THING ABOUT JAY WALKING HAS NOTHING TO DO WITH THEM, ALSO SOMETHING ABOUT THE PECKING ORDER.

BILHORN LIKES THE ONE ABOUT GIVING SOMEONE THE BIRD.

BEEKEE LIKES SINGING LIKE A BIRD. BK ENJOYS LISTENING TO THOSE WONDERFUL SINGERS WHO COULD SING LIKE CANARIES. YOU'VE PROBABLY HEARD OF SOME OF BK'S FAVORITES LIKE ELLA, LENA, DINAH, PATTI, SARAH, DORIS, MARY, JOAN, DONNA, AND JUDY. ARE ANY OF THESE YOUR FAVORITES?

43-- IT'S NOW A REAR STEAK

PEOPLE HAVE A PREFERENCE AS TO HOW THEIR MEAT IS COOKED. THE REAR STEAK IN THIS PICTURE HAS NOTHING TO DO WITH COOKING.

43— IT'S NOW A REAR STEAK

STEAKS ARE ORDERED WITH THE QUESTION, HOW RED?

WILL IT BE TOO RED?

DOES MEDIUM COME OUT RED IN THE MIDDLE?

DOES MEDIUM RARE COME VERY RED?

CAN MEDIUM WELL BE A LITTLE RED IN THE MIDDLE?

CAN IT BE A LITTLE RED BUT NOT PINK.

MAKE IT WELL DONE, NO RED.

WHEN THE WELL DONE MEAT IS DRY, RED STUFF FROM THE BOTTLE IS POURED OVER IT, MAKING IT A SEA OF RED THAT YOU CAN'T SEE THE MEAT.

THE VEGAN DOESN'T CAUSE THESE PROBLEMS.

THIS CARTOON LOOKED TO MAKE USE OF A NOT SO RARE HOMONYM.

THE TOONOLOGIST FEELS IT WAS WELL DONE.

THE PICTURE IS P. C.,   PERSONALLY CANNED

JUST DEBUNKED

THIS CARTOON COMES FROM LISTENING TO SOMEONE ON CABLE TELEVISION SAYING, IT WAS DEBUNKED. NOT EVERYONE AGREED THAT IT WAS DEBUNKED. THEY THOUGHT IT WAS NEVER DEBUNKED.
THIS CARTOON IS, JUST DEBUNKED.

44-- JUST DEBUNKED

IN THIS BOOK THERE ARE THREE BED CARTOONS. THERE'S THE MAN BED VETS, NEVER GETS OFF FROM THE WRONG SIDE AND JUST DEBUNKED.

THERE COULD BE MANY MORE BED CARTOONS, BUT THIS BOOK WILL NOT INCLUDE THAT TYPE OF MATERIAL.

ACTUALLY, IF YOU COUNT MY PILLOW CASE, IT'S FOUR BED CARTOONS.

ACTUALLY, IF YOU KEEP THINKING ABOUT MORE BED CARTOONS, THERE COULD BE A BED OF LETTUCE, A NUMBER BED, IT'S A HI-RISER BED, THIS IS A 7 FOOT BED, MAKING A BED, A RIVER BED, A WATER BED, IT'S BEDTIME AND IT'S NO BED OF ROSES. BUT FOR NOW WE WILL LET IT REST.

HE'S P. C., PREFERS CASUAL

45-- THE LATEST RAGE

THE LATEST RAGE

HERE, THE KID IS EXPERIENCING THE FATHER'S LATEST RAGE. LET'S HOPE THERE'S NO RAGE WHEN DEALING WITH CHILDREN. THE LATEST RAGE REFERS TO A NEW FAD AND RAGE SEEMS TO BE THE NEW FAD IN MANY CASES.

45-- THE LATEST RAGE

THERE'S RAGE ALL AROUND US, ROAD RAGE, PARENT RAGE, PROTESTER RAGE, GUN VIOLENCE RAGE EVEN POLITICAL RAGE. RAGE EXISTS AND IT'S SCARY.

THERE ARE DRIVERS THAT EXHIBIT RAGE AT OTHER DRIVERS FOR SAFE AND CAUTIOUS DRIVING. THE LIGHT JUST TURNS TO GREEN AND THE HORN FROM 3 CARS BEHIND GOES INTO PLAY. THERE COULD BE A PERSON CROSSING OR A YOUNGSTER ON A BIKE, SO WHAT, THE HORN GETS LONGER AND STRONGER.

WATCHING CABLE TELEVISION YOU CAN WITNESS SENATORS, THE MEN WITH SHIRTS AND TIES, BERATING WOMEN THAT ARE INVITED TO TESTIFY. MAYBE THE LATEST RAGE, THE NEW WAY IN CONGRESSIONAL HEARINGS, IS VERBAL RAGE.

IF SO THE LATEST RAGE IS SHAMEFUL.

LET'S BE P.C., PROVIDE COMPASSION

LONELY AT THE TOP

Lonely at the Top

THIS LINE WAS SPOKEN IN A MOVIE. PSYCHOLOGISTS DISCUSS THE REASONS FOR WHY IT'S LONELY AT THE TOP. IN THIS CARTOON LONELY AT THE TOP IS CLEAR.

46— LONELY AT THE TOP

THERE ARE MEN THAT UTILIZE A COUPLE OF STRANDS OF HAIR ON THEIR HEAD TO COVER THE COMPLETE TOP OF THEIR HEAD.

THEY MANEUVER A STRAND THAT SOMETIMES COULD BE MANY FEET LONG.

A GUY TELLS A STORY, WHILE PLAYING A POKER GAME HIS HAIR UNRAVELED ALLOWING A CAT TO GET HOLD OF IT, PULLING HIS HEAD BACK UNTIL THE CAT LET IT LOOSE.

TODAY MANY MEN SHAVE THEIR HEAD GETTING RID OF THE FINANCIAL BURDEN THAT HAIR CARE DEMANDS.

EVEN THOUGH THERE IS A STRAND OF HUMOR HERE, IT CAN BE A HAIRY TOPIC.

IF ASKED WHETHER YOU LIKE THIS CARTOON, PLEASE DON'T ANSWER, IT'S NEITHER HAIR NOR THERE.

THIS COMMENTARY IS P.C., PERSONAL COVERING.

47-- A MAN SEVERING ALL TIES

A MAN SEVERING ALL TIES

SEVERING ALL TIES CAN BE SOCIALLY DIFFICULT. TO COMPLETELY END A RELATIONSHIP OR HAVE A FINAL DETACHMENT FROM AN ASSOCIATION IS PROBABLY CAUSED BY UPSETTING ISSUES. WHEN THIS TOONOLOGIST HEARS CUTTING ALL TIES, IT'S SOMEONE WITH A SCISSOR.

47--   A MAN SEVERING ALL TIES

THE TOONOLOGIST WOULD ADVISE CUTTING ALL TIES WITH THE FOLLOWING:

USE OF ADDICTIVE DRUGS

SMOKING THOSE HARSH SMELLING CIGARETTES

NON-ACCEPTANCE OF FREE SPEECH

COMPLETE BIAS WITHOUT SELF EVALUATION

SELF PITY

RAGE

ON THE OTHER SIDE, DO NOT CUT TIES WITH:

SOAP

RESPECT FOR POLITICAL DISSENT

MOUTHWASH

ACCEPTANCE OF REASONABLE THINKING

LAUNDRY DETERGENT

THE TOONOLOGIST WOULD LIKE TO SEVER ALL TIES WITH TIES.

HERE IT'S P.C., --- PERSONAL CANDOR

48—NEWS, CALL FOR SANCTIONS

IT IS CONGRESS THAT VOTES FOR SANCTIONS AGAINST COUNTRIES THAT PROMOTE OR SPONSOR TERRORISM AND ANTI-SOCIAL BEHAVIOR.

48—NEWS, CALL FOR SANCTIONS

HERE AGAIN, CENTER STAGE IN THIS NEWSTOON INVOLVES REPRESENTATIVES OF CONGRESS.

SOME MIGHT SAY IT'S NOT CENTER STAGE, BUT BACK STAGE.

TOONS WOULD LIKE GETTING ON WITH THE COUNTRY'S BUSINESS, FUNDING THE MILITARY, FOCUSING ON THE INNER CITIES AND WORKING FOR PEOPLE TO BE PROUD, TO BE AMERICANS.

TOONS IS LOOKING FOR CONGRESS TO LEGISLATE TO A BETTER ATMOSPHERE AND A BETTER FUTURE FOR THE CITIZENS.

CABLE TELEVISION NEWS PROGRAMS DISCUSSED THAT YOU CAN'T LEAD FROM BEHIND.

A WAY FOR THIS NEWSTOON TO BE P.C., PREVENT CARCASSING.

49—BEEKEE AND BILHORN, ON THE FENCE

BEEKEE AND BILHORN ARE TALKING ABOUT THE EXPRESSION, HE'S SITTING ON THE FENCE. THEY KNOW IT MEANS HE CAN'T DECIDE BETWEEN 2 THINGS, BUT THE 2 BIRDS FEEL THAT THEY MAKE THEIR BEST DECISIONS, SITTING ON A FENCE.

49—BEEKEE AND BILHORN, ON THE FENCE

BECAUSE OF BEEKEE AND BILHORN, SO MUCH KNOWLEDGE HAS BEEN GAINED FROM THIS BOOK. BK AND BH HELPED TO RESEARCH HISTORY, GEOGRAPHY, CURRENT EVENTS, PROVERBS, IDIOMS AND GAVE US BIRD HUMOR.

ORGANIZING LISTS OF BIRD SONGS, MOVIES WITH BIRDS AND FAMOUS PEOPLE WITH BIRD NAMES TO ADD INFORMATION TO THE BIRDTOONS, MADE THE WRITING FUN.

BK AND BH WOULD LIKE TO ADD THEIR THOUGHTS ABOUT THE WALL, BUT IT WILL BECOME TOO POLITICAL.

BEEKEE AND BILHORN LIKE TO BE PERCHED HIGH, IT GIVES THEM GREAT VIEWS.

SOME FEEL SAFE BEHIND FENCES AND WALLS, BIRDS PROBABLY FEEL SAFER ON TOP OF THEM.

50—BEEKEE AND BILHORN, NOT YET BEGUN

BILHORN IS TELLING BEEKEE THAT THE EXACT WORDS ATTRIBUTED TO NAVY COMMANDER JOHN PAUL JONES WERE, "I HAVE NOT YET BEGUN TO FIGHT"

50-BEEKEE AND BILHORN, NOT YET BEGUN

COMMANDER J. P. JONES IS CONSIDERED THE FATHER OF THE AMERICAN NAVY.

DURING THE REVOLUTIONARY WAR HE WAS ASKED TO SURRENDER, HE REPLIED "I HAVE YET BEGUN TO FIGHT"

COMMANDER JONES SAILED WITH A CREW OF 140 MEN ON THE USS RANGER, LEAVING 4/10/1778 TO BEGIN RAIDS ON BRITISH WARSHIPS.

HE WAS BORN JOHN PAUL IN SCOTLAND AND ADDED JONES BECAUSE OF HIS ADMIRATION FOR WILLIE JONES, A PATRIOT OF NORTH CAROLINA.

BILHORN IS ASKING BEEKEE, DO YOU BELIEVE ALL THIS HAPPENED IN 1778?

DID A GUY BORN IN SCOTLAND HEAR ABOUT WILLIE IN CAROLINA, LEAVE FROM FRANCE IN 1778 TO FIGHT FOR AMERICA AGAINST THE BRITISH?

51—BEEKEE AND BILHORN,   MOVIES

B AND B BEING INTERESTED IN ALL THAT RELATES TO BIRDS, SUGGEST BIRD MOVIES BE IN THE BOOK. BILHORN MENTIONS SOME CLASSICS THAT MIGHT BE INCLUDED. BH IS CONSIDERING MOVIES ABOUT BIRDS AND EVEN MOVIES WITH BIRD WORDS IN THE TITLE.

51—BEEKEE AND BILHORN, MOVIES

THERE ARE PLENTY OF MOVIES INVOLVING BIRDS, THE LIST COULD FILL A BOOK.

HERE ARE SOME OF B AND B'S FAVORITES:

HOWARD THE DUCK

RIO

FOLLOW THAT BIRD

ASTRONUT WOODY

UGLY DUCKLING

CHICKEN LITTLE

YANKEE DOODLE DAFFY

DAFFY DUCK IN HOLLYWOOD

TWEETY'S ADVENTURES

MY LITTLE DUCKAROO

BEEKEE AND BILHORN ENJOY WATCHING A FUNNY DUCK OR WOODY MOVIE, WHILE PECKING AWAY ON SOME POPCORN.

MEN OF STEAL

SHOPLIFTING WAS IN THE NEWS BIGTIME WHEN COLLEGE BASKETBALL PLAYERS REMOVED PRICEY SUNGLASSES FROM A STORE IN CHINA.

MEN OF STEAL

TO SOME SHOPLIFTING IS AN ART. THE PROCEDURE CAN BE WELL PLANNED. SOMETIMES MORE THAN ONE PERSON IS INVOLVED IN THE LIFT. AN ADULT USES A CHILD TO GAIN THE EDGE.

AS FAR AS THE BASKETBALL PLAYERS, PROBABLY ALL EYES WERE ON THEM BECAUSE OF THEIR SIZE.

THE STORY BECAME BIG AFTER THE PRESIDENT WORKED OUT THEIR RELEASE FROM JAIL.

IT WAS PUBLICIZED BECAUSE OF THE TYPE OF THANKS AND THE DISTURBING EVALUATION OF THE INCIDENT GIVEN BY THOSE INVOLVED.

MANY IDEAS COME TO THE TOONOLOGIST'S CRANIUM. MAYBE THE SHOPLIFTERS SHOULD BE ALLOWED FREE LIFT TICKETS AND SHOP OWNERS TO WRAP THE LOOT. TOONS DEEMS THESE PERMISSIVE ATTITUDES A STAIN ON OUR FAMILY VALUES AND OUR EMPHASIS ON MORALITY. HERE'S THE P.C., --- PRISON CANDIDATES

NEVER GETS OFF WRONG

NEVER GETS OFF THE WRONG SIDE OF THE BED

THERE IS SUCH A THING AS MORNING GRUMPINESS. WHEN SOMEONE ENCOUNTERS THIS PERSON, THEY SAY HEY, GOT UP ON THE WRONG SIDE OF THE BED.
PUT ONE SIDE AGAINST THE WALL AND NEVER GET OFF THE WRONG SIDE.

53— NEVER GETS OFF WRONG

THERE ARE BOSSES THAT ARE WRONG SIDE OF THE BED PEOPLE.

THERE ARE BOSSES THAT MAKE IT COMFORTABLE FOR WORKERS ARRIVING EACH MORNING.

ADMINISTRATORS, SUPERVISORS SHOULD BE THRILLED WHEN WORKERS APPEAR FOR WORK.

IN EVERY PLACE THERE ARE THOSE WHO NEVER SMILE. EVEN WHEN THEY GREET SOMEONE, IT'S A GREETING WITHOUT A SMILE.

THERE ARE BOTTLES OF PILLS AND TABLETS FOR EVERYTHING, THERE SHOULD BE A PILL THAT PUTS A SMILE ON, WHEN SPEAKING WITH PEOPLE.

THE TOONOLOGIST SMILED WHEN WRITING 101 CARTOONS, AND HOPES IT BRINGS SOME SMILES TO YOU.

WE WANT P.C.,   PROVIDE COMFORT

54—NEWS, NO FLY ZONE

MILITARY ISSUES CAN RESULT IN NO FLY ZONE SITUATIONS. THERE WAS AN AIRCRAFT BAN OVER IRAQ FOR YEARS. THE UNITED NATIONS BANNED PLANES OVER LIBYA IN 2011. WHEN SOME COUNTRIES DON'T AGREE TO THE NO FLY ZONE, IT'S A SCARY SKY UP THERE.

54—NEWS, NO FLY ZONE

LET'S MENTION 3 NO FLY ZONE ISSUES.

ONE IS THE MILITARY GUARDING AIR SPACE IN A CONFLICT ZONE.

TWO IS THE ATTEMPT TO LIMIT BIRDS FROM INTERFERING WITH AIRCRAFT NEAR AIRPORTS. THE NUMBER OF BIRDS COLLIDING WITH PLANES IS ASTOUNDING.

THERE WERE 10,700 BIRD STRIKES IN ONE YEAR AROUND 2013.

BIRD EXPERTS ARE EMPLOYED TO ALERT AIRPORTS ABOUT BAD BIRD SITUATIONS.

THE USE OF LASERS, SOUND EQUIPMENT AND OTHER BIRD CONTROL TECHNIQUES MINIMIZE THE DANGER OF BIRDS BEING SUCKED INTO ENGINES.

THREE IS THE CARTOON PICTURE, AS THEY SWAT THE PESTY FLIES AND MOSQUITOS AWAY.

IT IS ANNOYING AT A PICNIC OR DINNER IF YOU SPEND HALF THE TIME SLAPPING YOURSELF EVERYTIME A BUG BITES YOUR LEG, NECK OR NOSE.

THE CARTOON IS P.C., PEST CONTROL

55— NO JUMPING TO CONCLUSIONS

NO JUMPING TO CONCLUSIONS

THE TOPIC OF THIS CARTOON MAY MAKE IT THE MOST IMPORTANT ONE IN THE BOOK. WHO IS ALWAYS PREJUDGING AND THINKING THEY ARE SMART?

55— NO JUMPING TO CONCLUSIONS

IN THE PAST COUPLE OF YEARS, TELEVISION NEWS WAS BOMBARDED WITH PREJUDGMENTS. THERE WILL BE NONE OF IT HERE, JUST QUESTIONS.

DO YOU JUDGE BEFORE YOU KNOW THE FACTS?

DO YOU PREJUDGE BECAUSE YOU ARE EXTRA SMART?

DO YOU ENJOY BEING INCORRECT?

DO YOU ADMIT WHEN YOU ARE INCORRECT?

DO YOU CHANGE YOUR ORIGINAL WRONG ANSWER?

DO YOU PREJUDGE AS PART OF A GROUP?

DO YOU PREJUDGE AND SHOOT OUT NASTY LABELS?

RECENTLY INDIVIDUAL STUDENTS WERE ASKED THEIR OPINION ON A NATIONAL SPEECH. EACH ONE GAVE IT A BIG NEGATIVE.

LATER THEY WERE TOLD THAT THE SPEECH WAS NOT YET GIVEN, IT WAS SCHEDULED FOR THE NEXT DAY.

DOES PREJUDGING POINT TO SOME KIND OF BIAS?

AUTOMATIC P.C.,   PREJUDGING COMPLICATES

OF COURSE, THEY SUPPORT WOMEN

THIS IS WHAT HAPPENED. HERE IT IS, SOME POLITICIANS TAKING MATTERS INTO THEIR OWN HANDS, WHILE THEY CLAIM SUPPORTING WOMEN.

56—NEWS,   SUPPORTING   WOMEN

IT'S BIG NEWS NOW, THE SUPPORT FOR WOMEN IS COMING FROM ALL DIRECTIONS.

PEOPLE THAT BEAT UP ON THE WOMEN WHO ACCUSED MEN OF ABUSING THEM, ARE NOW PROMOTING WOMEN SUPPORT.

PEOPLE THAT STUCK WITH THE ABUSERS ARE NOW THINKING TO SUPPORT THE ACCUSERS.

BECAUSE TOONS SUPPORTS PROPER TREATMENT OF WOMEN, THERE WILL BE MORE WOMEN'S SUPPORT NEWSTOONS PRINTED IN THIS BOOK.

TOONS WANTS THIS ISSUE OUT IN THE OPEN AND NOT HIDDEN ON THE BACK BURNER. EVEN THOUGH IT'S A TOUCHY ISSUE, DEALING WITH IT UP FRONT SHOULD HAVE IT WELL IN HAND.

WE NEED P.C.,   PENALIZED CONTACT

ONE-TON SOUP

WHEN A TOONOLOGIST HEARS SOME WORDS THAT FORM A PICTURE OR A THOUGHT, IT CAN WIND UP A CARTOON. WONTON SOUP, ENJOYED BY MANY, IS CONSUMED BY THE TON EVERYDAY.
SO HERE ONE TON OF SOUP FILLS AN ABOVE GROUND POOL.

57-- ONE TON SOUP

IN THE POOL THERE'S ONE TON OF SOUP. THERE ARE NO WONTONS, NO PIECES OF CHICKEN OR PORK, ONLY ONE-TON SOUP.

THE TOONOLOGIST WOULD RATHER HAVE HOT AND SOUR SOUP, BUT IT DIDN'T FIT WELL IN THE CARTOON.

IF YOU IMMEDIATELY THOUGHT OF WONTON SOUP WHEN YOU SAW THE CARTOON TITLE, THE IDEA HIT THE SPOT, JUST LIKE A GOOD BOWL OF WONTON SOUP.

YOU COULD PROBABLY SET UP CARTOONS OF YOUR OWN, IF YOU IMMEDIATELY THOUGHT WONTON SOUP.

YOUR FOOD CARTOONS COULD BE PIGS IN A BLANKET, SHOE FLY PIE, 3 FOOT HEROES OR HOT DOGS.

IF YOUR FAVORITE IS HOT BUNS, WATCHOUT.

FIRST GO OUT AND ENJOY A GOOD BOWL OF SOUP.

CAN THIS BE P.C.?   POPULAR CHOICE

58— THE ONE WHO PULLS THE STRINGS

THE ONE WHO PULLS THE STRINGS

PEOPLE THAT REPEAT THIS IDIOM ARE TALKING ABOUT SOMEONE THAT IS IN CHARGE, SOME PERSON AT THE HELM, OR WHO IS IN THE POSITION CONTROLLING THE WHOLE SHABANG.

58— THE ONE WHO PULLS THE STRINGS

THE HEADS OF COMPANIES ARE PEOPLE WHO PULL THE STRINGS. SOME USE THEIR INFLUENCE WITH COMPASSION, SOME ARE ONLY KNOWN FOR TAKING ADVANTAGE OF THEIR POSITION.

FOR MANY YEARS PEOPLE SAID THAT A STATE IN THE EAST, WAS CONTROLLED BY A FEW PEOPLE. THEY WERE THE ONES PULLING THE STRINGS. IF A PERSON COMPLAINED ABOUT THE STRING PULLER, THE STRINGS COULD FIGURATIVELY BE WOUND AROUND THE COMPLAINER'S NECK. THERE ARE SOME TERRIFIC AND APPLAUDED STRING PULLERS.

THE CHILD THAT LEARNS TO TIE THE SHOE LACES, THE MEDICAL PEOPLE THAT STITCH UP WOUNDS. THE PEOPLE THAT WOUND STRING AROUND BOXES THAT MADE IT EASIER TO CARRY AND OF COURSE A PUPPETEER.

IT'S GOOD TO THINK POSITIVE.

HOW DO YOU EXPLAIN WOUND(HURT) AND WOUND(STRING) PRONOUNCED DIFFERENTLY?

THIS IS THE P.C.,   POLITICAL CONTROL

PASSING STOP SIGNS

PASSING STOP SIGNS

PASSING STOP SIGNS RESULTS IN NASTY CAR ACCIDENTS AT STREET CORNERS IN THE BOROUGHS OF NEW YORK CITY.
FOR EVERY ACCIDENT THERE ARE PROBABLY 10,000 CLOSE CALLS.

59--   PASSING STOP SIGNS

HERE ARE A FEW STOP SIGN ACCIDENTS, PERSONALLY OBSERVED ON THE STREET CORNER.

A LOUD NOISE ALERTED ME TO WALK TO THE SCENE. A YOUNG MAN WHO PASSED THE STOP SIGN WAS ON HIS WAY TO THE INSURANCE AGENT TO PAY FOR HIS CAR INSURANCE POLICY. HE WAS ANXIOUS TO BE ON THE ROAD LEGALLY.

WHEN I WAS WALKING HOME I SAW 2 POLICEMEN LIFTING A REAR CAR DOOR, LOOKING TO PLACE IT INTO THE BACK SEAT OF THE CAR. THE SMASHED CARS REMAINED ON THE STREET BUT THE DRIVERS WERE NOT IN SIGHT. PASSING A STOP SIGN CAN RESULT IN A LONG HOSPITAL STAY.

ON A THANKSGIVING DAY A DRIVER PASSED THE SIGN, HIT THE BRAKES AND BANGED INTO MY FENDER. HE SAID THAT HE WAS RUSHING TO GET TO HIS DAUGHTER. I WENT ON MY WAY BUT HE COULDN'T GET THE HOOD OF HIS CAR BACK INTO POSITION. HE PROBABLY MISSED THE COCKTAIL HOUR.

MAYBE A NEW ADDITION TO CARS COULD BE A STOP SIGN SENSOR SAYING, STOP IN THE NAME OF THE LAW.

P. C., PROCEED CAUTIOUSLY

60—NEWS, PERKS, NO! JERKS, YES!

PERKS NO! - JERKS YES!

AGAIN, IT WAS THE NEWS THAT PROMPTED THESE CONGRESSIONAL POSITION CARTOONS. CONGRESS DOES RECEIVE A NICE SET OF PERKS. THIS IS NOT AN ACCEPTABLE ONE.

60—NEWS,   PERKS, NO!   JERKS, YES!

WHEN CONGRESS IS IN SESSION THE PERKS INCLUDE THE GYM, THE POOL AND TENNIS.

THE AMERICAN CITIZENS ARE PROUD, PARTLY FOR AFFORDING THEIR REPRESENTATIVE THE BEST.

THEY ARE GIVEN SPECIAL TREATMENT BY THE AIRLINES, WHICH INCLUDES FREE AIRPORT PARKING.

TOONS FEELS THAT ACTIVE MILITARY SHOULD BE GIVEN AIRLINE PERKS.

HOPEFULLY THE REPRESENTATIVES APPRECIATE THEIR CONSTITUENTS AND THE PERK THAT IS THE OPPORTUNITY FOR DOING GOOD THINGS FOR THE PEOPLE.

WHILE PUTTING THIS BOOK TOGETHER THERE WERE MORE RESIGNATIONS FROM THE POLITICAL AND MEDIA ESTABLISHMENT WHEN ACCUSED OF ACTIONS BENEATH SOCIAL ACCEPTANCE.

THE PICTURE, NOT P.C.,   PERSISTANTLY CRASS

61—BEEKEE AND BILHORN, DON'T LET THE CAT OUT

IF YOU READ ABOUT CATS AND BIRDS, YOU KNOW THAT CATS KILL A BILLION BIRDS A YEAR. SO BIRDS WOULD RATHER CATS STAY IN THE BAG.

61—BEEKEE AND BILHORN, DON'T LET THE CAT OUT

THE LIST OF EVERYDAY PREDATORS LOOKING TO GET BIRDS INCLUDES OPOSSUMS, SKUNKS, FOXES, DOGS AS WELL AS CATS.

SMALL BIRDS ARE DEFENSELESS. THEY CAN RETREAT BUT HAVE NO OFFENSIVE WEAPONS.

THEIR LITTLE BEAKS SHOULD BE WEAPONIZED INTO A BEAK BELTER. WHEN THE BEAK POKES THE BACKSIDE OF A BIGGER ANIMAL IT SHOULD RESULT IN A K.O. SO THE ANIMAL FALLS TO THE GROUND HELPLESS.

PREDATORS WOULD THINK TWICE BEFORE GOING ANYWHERE NEAR THE BIRD.

WHAT A SCENE IT WOULD BE IF A BIRD POKED A FEROCIOUS ANIMAL INTO SUBMISSION. THIS IS WHY IT'S A CARTOON BOOK.

THE IDIOM FREE AS A BIRD, IS NOT ACCURATE WHEN IT COMES TO BIRD SURVIVAL.

62—BEEKEE AND BILHORN, THE FLU SHOT

HERE YOU GET A BIT OF THE BIRDS' SENSE OF HUMOR. THESE BIRDS ARE HAPPY EVEN THOUGH IT'S A CONTINUOUS SEARCH FOR FOOD AND SHELTER.

62—BEEKEE AND BILHORN,   THE FLU SHOT

VERY SERIOUS IS THE FLU EPIDEMIC THIS SEASON.

THEY SAY THE FLU SHOT IS LESS THAN 30% EFFECTIVE.

TOONS HAS NO IDEA OF WHAT THAT MEANS, JUST THAT TOO MANY PEOPLE HAVE BEEN HIT WITH THE FLU BUG CAUSING ILLNESS AND DEATH. THE 2 BIRDS WILL NOT TAKE INJECTIONS.

DID YOU KNOW THAT THERE ARE PEOPLE THAT FEAR FEATHERS? IT'S CALLED PTERONOPHOBIA. IT SEEMS THAT BEING TICKLED WITH A FEATHER IS SCARY TO SOME. GIVING THE BIRDS A SENSE OF HUMOR IS NOT TOO FAR FETCHED, IT'S FOR A CARTOON BOOK.

THERE ARE SOME FUNNY BIRDS IN CARTOONS.

THERE ARE EVEN SOME FUNNY BIRD JOKES.

GOING INTO THE PET SHOP TO BUY A BIRD THAT SINGS.

SO HERE'S A BIRD, LIFT ITS LEFT LEG IT SINGS AMERICA, LIFT ITS RIGHT LEG IT SINGS THE ANTHEM. WHAT IF YOU LIFT BOTH LEGS? BIRD YELLS, I'LL FALL ON MY ---!

63—BEEKEE AND BILHORN, F. NIGHTINGALE

THE BOOK CHARACTERS IN THE BIRDTOON ARE MEDICAL STAFFERS. THEY WILL FLY WHEREVER NEEDED. ALL 3 HAVE SPECIAL SKILLS.

63—BEEKEE AND BILHORN, F. NIGHTINGALE

F. NIGHTINGALE IS WORLD RENOWN FOR HER TREATING SOLDIERS INJURED AT WAR AND ESTABLISHING A NURSING SCHOOL.

SHE WAS GIVEN THE NAME THE LADY WITH THE LAMP WHEN SHE MADE HER ROUNDS DURING THE NIGHT.

BIRD ANNIE AND BIRD DANIELLE ARE ALWAYS KNOWN FOR SPECIALIZING IN CARING FOR THE YOUNG.

BIRD DANIELLE CAN SPOT AND IDENTIFY A BIRD IN THICKEST TREES.

IN BILHORN'S BIRD BOOK THE MEDICAL STAFF MUST ALWAYS BE ON CALL.

LIKE ANY HOSPITAL THE BIRDS ARE EVALUATED IN THE TREE-AJHE AREA.

64—NEWS,   HAVE WOMEN'S BACK

POLI**TUCHANS** THAT HAVE THE WOMEN'S BACK

THEY'RE BACK AGAIN. SO MANY WOMEN SAY THAT THEY FELT THE PRESSURE OF MEN'S BAD INTENTIONS. THEY FELT MENTAL PRESSURE OR MAYBE THE PRESSURE IN THE PICTURE.

64—NEWS, HAVE WOMEN'S BACK

AS WRITTEN IN THE INTRODUCTION, NO NAMES, NO PARTIES, NO BIAS IS CONTAINED IN THIS BOOK, JUST GENERAL AREAS CARTOONED ABOUT PRIVATE AREAS.

THE TOONS ARE PRESENTED TO BRING A SMILE AND SOME THOUGHT.

IF YOU PAY ATTENTION TO NEWS REPORTING, IT MAY INFLUENCE YOUR WAY OF THINKING OF THE PICTURE.

IT'S ALSO POSSIBLE THAT YOU LOOK AND THINK OF THE PICTURE WITHOUT MEDIA INFLUENCE.

PEOPLE CAN HAVE A DIFFERENT VIEW OF THE SAME NEWSTOON.

POSSIBLY THEY REFUSE THAT THIS OCCURS, OR JUST LOOK AT IT WITH DISGUST, OR MAYBE THEY SAY IT'S VERY WELL DONE.

JUST LIKE ANY OTHER PIECE OF ART IT'S IN THE HANDS OF THE BEHOLDER.

IT IS PROBLEMATIC P.C., PROBLEMATIC CONCEPT

65—NEWS, HAND IN HAND

OFTEN WHEN A JOB OR PROJECT IS COMPLETED IN SUPERB FASHION, SOME SPEAK ABOUT WORKING HAND IN HAND. HERE YOU'RE WITNESSING SARCASM.

65—NEWS,   HAND IN HAND

TODAY'S CONGRESS IS NOT KNOWN FOR WORKING HAND IN HAND. TOONS DOES NOT LAY BLAME, JUST ECHOING THE GENERAL PUBLIC RATING.

THIS BOOK HAS THE ONE WHO PULLS THE STRINGS CARTOON, MANY THINK CONGRESS IS AN EXAMPLE OF THAT CARTOON.

ONE CONGRESS PERSON WAS ON TELEVISION COMPLAINING THAT 2 PEOPLE HAVE SO MUCH POWER. THE FACT IS THAT THE COMPLAINER WENT RIGHT ALONG, FOLLOWING THE STRING PULLERS.

THESE ARE HIGHLY EDUCATED PEOPLE THAT WILL SAY ANYTHING THE STRING PULLERS PUSH.

AT TIMES THEY ARE WORKING HAND IN HAND.

THEY WORK HAND IN HAND TO STAY ON THE GOOD SIDE OF THE STRING PULLERS.

ARE YOUR STRINGS BEING PULLED?

YOU HAVE P.C.,   POMPOUS CONDUCT

THE PROOF'S IN THE PUDDING

THE PROOF IS IN THE PUDDING

ORIGINALLY IT WAS THE PROOF OF THE PUDDING IS IN THE EATING. IT WAS EATEN TO SEE IF IT PASSED THE TEST. NOW IT'S THE PROOF IS IN THE PUDDING. HERE IT'S 90 PROOF THAT'S PUT INTO THE PUDDING.

66— THE PROOF'S IN THE PUDDING

THERE IS QUITE A LONG LIST OF PUDDINGS THAT ARE SERVED OVER THE WORLD. WIKIPEDIA OFFERS AN INTERESTING LIST OF DESSERTS AND THEIR COUNTRY WHERE FIRST SERVED.

BIG ON PUDDINGS IS THE UNITED KINGDOM. THEY ENJOY EATING YORKSHIRE, FIGGY, DOCK, RAG, CHRISTMAS, AND BREAD AND BUTTER PUDDING.

PUDDINGS FROM THE U.S.A. ARE PERSIMMON, COCONUT BREAD, COTTAGE AND BANANA PUDDING.

THE ORIGINS OF RICE, TAPIOCA AND CHOCOLATE PUDDINGS WERE NOT FOUND.

PUDDINGS SERVED IN OTHER COUNTRIES AROUND THE WORLD ARE MANGO, MALVA, RED AND LANGEVINGER. HAVE YOU TASTED ANY OF THESE?

TOON THINKS IF THE PROOF IS PUT INTO THE PUDDINGS, DO NOT SERVE THEM TO THE YOUNG.

P. C.,-----PUTTING CALORIES

THE PROTESTEES

THERE ARE PROTESTS AGAINST PEOPLE, STORES, COUNTRIES, IDEAS, LOGOS, WORDS AND PROTESTORS. THERE ARE PROTESTORS FOR FREE SPEECH THAT LOOK TO BAN SPEAKERS. THERE ARE PROTESTEES.

67-- THE PROTESTEES

THERE ARE PROTESTS AGAINST HIGH CRIME.

THERE ARE PROTESTS AGAINST STOP AND FRISK.

THERE ARE CALLS FOR MORE POLICE.

THERE ARE PROTESTS AGAINST POLICE.

THERE ARE RALLIES PETITIONING AGAINST UNSAFE STREETS.

THEY PROTEST FOR FREEDOM OF SPEECH. POPULAR SEEMS TO BE PROTESTERS FOR FREE SPEECH, PROTESTING AGAINST SPEAKERS SPEAKING.

THERE'S THE PROTESTERS FOR FREEDOM OF ASSEMBLY, THAT PROTEST AGAINST THE MILITARY APPEARING ON CAMPUS TO RECRUIT FOR JOINING THE MILITARY.

FINALLY, VERY LOUD IS AN OUTCRY FOR FREEDOM TO BURN OUR FLAG. WOULD YOU LIKE TO PROTEST?

THIS CARTOON SHOWS A GROUP PROTESTING AGAINST ALL PROTESTERS, CALLED THE PROTESTEES.

WHAT IS YOUR THINKING ABOUT THIS P.C.?

PROTESTEES   COMPLAINTS

RAISING JOHN'S MARK

RAISING JOHN'S MARK

JOHN ASKED FOR HIS MARK TO BE RAISED. SO THE TEACHER MOVED THE 45 FROM THE LOWER PLACE TO A HIGHER PLACE ON THE TEST PAPER, SAYING WITH STUDY YOU CAN RAISE YOUR MARK.

RAISING JOHN'S MARK

IN EVERY ORGANIZATION THERE ARE PEOPLE WHO THINK THEY ARE FUNNY. THERE ARE SOME FUNNY TEACHERS AND ALSO TRICKY ONES. THEY USE TRICKS TO NEUTRALIZE A STUDENT THAT IS A TROUBLEMAKER. THEY ADMINISTER SOME EXPERIENCE TACTICS, APPLYING STRESS TO THE STUDENT. WHEN TEST PAPERS ARE RETURNED TO THE STUDENTS, ONE STUDENT'S TEST PAPER IS KEPT BY THE TEACHER, WITH THAT STUDENT TOLD THE PENALTY FOR NOT HANDING IN A TEST PAPER. PLACE AN UNUSUAL ITEM IN THE STUDENTS DESK. THEN CALL THE DEAN TO CHECK THE DESK WHEN THAT STUDENT IS SEATED AT THE DESK. THE TEACHER HAS A SERIOUS LOOK AS THE STUDENT IS PLEADING INNOCENCE TO THE DEAN.

TEACHERS WHO USE UNCONVENTIONAL STRATEGIES CAN GET A SMILE WHEN TELLING CLASSROOM STORIES TO FRIENDS AND COLLEAGUES.

WOULD YOU THINK OF HANGING A PICTURE OF THE DEAN AND SEATING THAT STUDENT FACING THE PICTURE AS A STRATEGY FOR DISCIPLINE?

WHY IS THIS P.C.?

PEACEFUL CLASSROOM

69—BEEKEE AND BILHORN, TAILGATING

TAILGATING IS PROBABLY THE CAUSE OF 90% OF MORNING DRIVE CAR ACCIDENTS. JUST ONE ACCIDENT CAN RESULT IN THOUSANDS OF PEOPLE SPENDING EXTRA HOURS ON THE ROAD.

69-- BEEKEE AND BILHORN, TAILGATING

THIS TOONOLOGIST HAS HAD 3 TAILGATING EXPERIENCES. EACH TIME IT HAPPENED WHEN STOPPED AT A RED LIGHT.

AFTER I STOPPED FOR THE RED LIGHT, THE CAR BEHIND MY CAR STOPPED ONLY AFTER HITTING MY REAR END.

THIS TIME THE CAR WAS APPROACHING MY CAR GOING OVER THE SPEED LIMIT.

NEXT TIME, THE CAR WAS GOING TOO FAST WITH THE INFLUENCE OF ALCOHOL.

TIME 3, THE DRIVER HAD TO CHOOSE TO LOOK AT THE ROAD OR THE PHONE. HE CHOSE THE PHONE.

LUCKILY NOBODY WAS HURT IN EITHER ACCIDENT.

THERE WAS VERY LITTLE DAMAGE AND AFTER POLICE REPORTS, ALL WENT ON THEIR WAY.

BEEKEE AND BILHORN GET A BIRDS EYE VIEW OF THE DAILY TRAFFIC.

THEY ARE LABELING TAILGATERS, AS THE BIRDBRAINS.

70—BEEKEE AND BILHORN, GIVING THE BIRD

BK AND BH HEARD THAT PEOPLE OFTEN GIVE OTHER PEOPLE THE BIRD. THE 2 BIRDS ARE ASKING, WHAT KIND OF BIRD IS GIVEN? IS IT A GIFT? IS IT GIVEN TO BE A PET?

70—BEEKEE AND BILHORN, GIVING THE BIRD

DRIVERS ARE NOT ALWAYS COURTEOUS. THEIR TEMPERS SOMETIMES GET OUT OF CONTROL. TOONS WOULD LIKE TO SEE A DRIVING HABIT REVOLUTION.

A RETURN TO DOING THE DRIVING THINGS THAT EARNED THEM A PASSING MARK WHEN THEY WERE AWARDED THE DRIVER'S LICENSE.

LET'S HAVE A PROGRAM THAT HELPS ELIMINATE ROAD RAGE AND THE GIFT OF GIVING THE BIRD.

IN THIS BOOK THERE'S RAGE FROM A PARENT TO A KID. THERE'S RAGE FROM A SENATOR AT A HEARING AND FROM A PEDESTRIAN THAT STEPS IN DOG STUFF. TOONS FEELS THIS LAST ONE WARRANTS RAGE. FOR THE OTHERS, INSTEAD OF RAGE, MAYBE GIVING THE BIRD WOULD BE FINE.

71—BEEKEE AND BILHORN, CANARY ISLANDS

THE 2 BIRDS ARE READING BROCHURES FOR POSSIBLE VACATIONS. THEY THOUGHT IT WOULD BE NICE TO FLY TO SOME PLACES WITH FRIENDLY NAMES. BEEKEE AND BILHORN CAN TWEET SOME SPANISH.

71—BEEKEE AND BILHORN, CANARY ISLANDS

BK AND BH FOUND THE CANARY ISLANDS TO BE VERY INTERESTING. THE 2 BIRDS GOT INFORMATION ABOUT BIRDS, OFFERED BY WIKIPEDIA.

THEY READ ABOUT TWO TYPES OF CANARIES, THE DOMESTICATED SINGING PET AND THE WILD CANARY.

THE ATLANTIC CANARY, ALSO CALLED THE WILD CANARY IS NATIVE TO THE CANARY ISLANDS.

THEY BELONG TO THE FINCH FAMILY. THE WILD ONE IS NOT PET MATERIAL.

THE CANARY ISLANDS INCLUDE 7 MAJOR ISLANDS AND A SET OF SMALLER ISLANDS.

B AND B WOULD LIKE TO VISIT TEIDE NATIONAL PARK AND GET TO SEE AND HEAR THEIR BIRD FRIENDS.

THEY MIGHT GET TO SEE TRUMPETER FINCH, STONECHAT, GOLDCREST, TURTLE DOVES, LAUGHING DOVES, PIGEONS; QUAIL AND MORE.

THE 2 BIRDS WILL BE IN THE AIR ABOUT 3,300 MILES.

72—NEWS, REACHING FOR THE STARS

REACHING FOR THE STARS

MORE NEWS IS BAD NEWS. THIS SHOULD BE THE LAST TOON INVOLVING THEATRICS.

72—NEWS,   REACHING FOR THE STARS

THIS CARTOON BOOK, THAT FEATURES SAYINGS, EXPRESSIONS, IDIOMS, PROVERBS AND SUCH, HAS THE TOONOLOGIST FILLED WITH VISUAL IMAGES.

REACHING FOR THE STARS PLUS ALL THE 2017 NEWS REPORTS PUTS A PICTURE LIKE THIS FRONT AND CENTER.

THIS BOOK STARTED OUT TO BE A JUST FOR FUN ENDEAVOR, BUT AFTER TURNING THE TELEVISION ON TO WATCH AND RELAX, THE BOMBS STARTED BURSTING WITH ONE REPORT AFTER ANOTHER FOCUSING ON SOME CONTEMPTUOUS BEHAVIOR.

IT FOSTERED THE THOUGHT OF A LARGE NUMBER OF NEWSTOONS. EVERYDAY THESE SUBJECTS WERE DISCUSSED. TOONS THOUGHT THIS MUST BE BROUGHT TO AN ACCEPTABLE END.

A WAY FOR THIS TO BE P.C.,   PROMOTE CONSTRAINT

73-- A ROLL CALL

A ROLL CALL

RECENTLY CONGRESS WAS CONDUCTING A ROLL CALL. HERE COMES AN EASY GOING CARTOON. IT MAKES ME THINK OF MY NEIGHBORHOOD BAKERY ROLL CALL AND THE NICE BAKERY AROMAS.

73--   A ROLL CALL

THE CONGRESSIONAL ROLL CALL INVOLVED BIG TIME LAPSES WHEN NO NAMES WERE BEING CALLED.

IN THE ARMY ROLL CALL DIDN'T HAVE DELAYS. THE NAME WAS CALLED, THE RESPONSE HEARD LOUD AND CLEAR, ONE AFTER ANOTHER.

IN THE BAKERY THE ROLL CALL IS SLOW AND PRECISE. TWO CRISP ROLLS WITH POPPY SEEDS, FOUR ROLLS WELL BAKED, SIX ONION ROLLS AND A JELLY ROLL. THAT SHOULD BE AN EVEN DOZEN PLUS 1.

IN RESTAURANTS ROLLS ARE PLACED ON THE TABLE BEFORE ORDERING THE MEAL. YOU ARE GIVEN SWEET ROLLS, DINNER ROLLS, ONION ROLLS, NICELY SUPPLIED.

THERE'S NOTHING LIKE A SUB OR HERO OR A HOAGIE ROLL HAVING THAT GOOD STUFF IN IT.

CAN BE CALLED P.C., ---PLEASANT CHEWING

A ROYAL FLUSH

ROYAL FLUSH

HOPEFULLY YOU DON'T THINK THIS TOO COARSE. BUTT IT HAPPENS IN EVERY PALACE ALL OVER THE WORLD.

74-- A ROYAL FLUSH

THE FIRST WEEK IN THE ARMY WAS SORT OF EMBARRASSING BECAUSE OF THE OPENESS OF THE BARRICKS BATHROOM.

SO TRYING TO AVOID BEING EMBARRASSED, YOU SNEAKED OFF TO THE BATHROOM AT 2 A.M. JUST TO FIND PLENTY OF OTHERS DOING THE SAME.

TO MANY THE BATHROOM IS A READING, A THINKING, EVEN A ROOM FOR SINGING AND OF COURSE A PLACE FOR HEALTH CARE.

THE AVERAGE 5X8 FEET BATHROOM COSTS ABOUT $10,000 TO RENOVATE. SOME CAN SPEND MULTIPLE THOUSANDS OF $$$$$ FOR A MAGNIFICENT BATHROOM.

TOONS LEAVES THE NEXT SENTENCE TO YOUR CREATIVE THINKING.

THIS SHOULD BE P.C., PERSONAL COMFORT

THE SKI PATROL

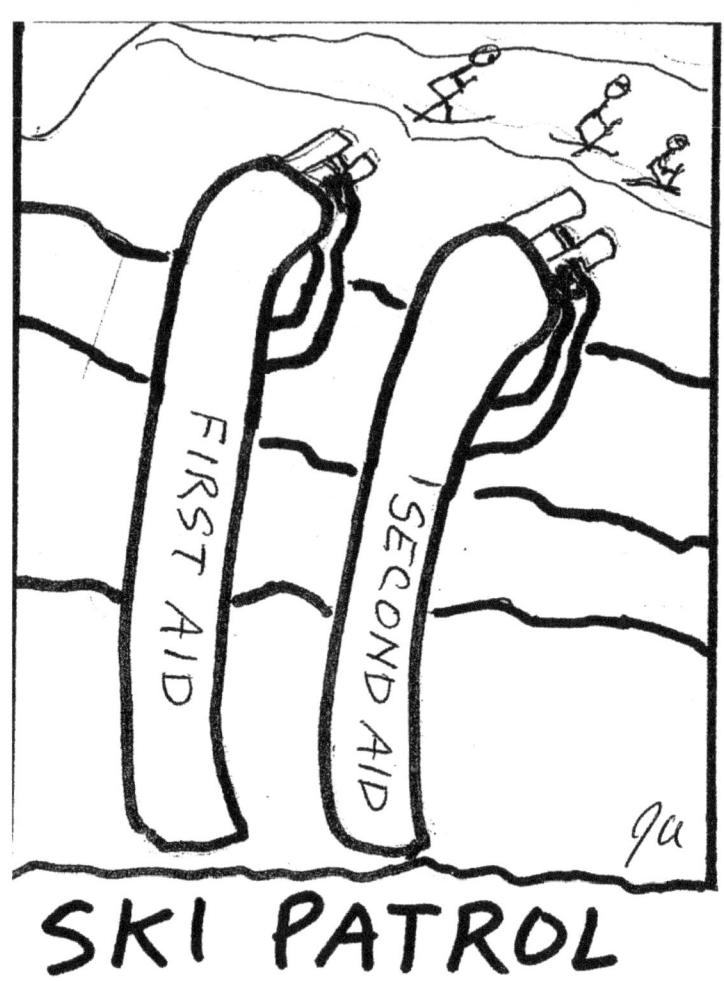

SKI PATROL

ON TOP OF A SKI SLOPE THE WINTER SCENE IS MAGNIFICENT. SKIING CAN BE BREATHTAKING. GETTING THAT SIGHT OF THE MOUNTAIN IS A JOY. AT TIMES ANOTHER GREAT SIGHT IS THE SKI PATROL.

75-- THE SKI PATROL

BROKEN LIMBS AND CONCUSSIONS ARE COMMON WHEN THERE ARE ACCIDENTS ON SKIS.

THE NAMES OF FAMOUS PEOPLE HURT OR EVEN WORSE WHEN ON SKIS INCLUDES MICHAEL, SONNY, CAROLINE, ARNOLD, HEATHER, MICHAEL AND ARA.

TRY THESE THREE C'S WHEN ON SKIS.

CAUTION

CAREFUL

CONSIDERATION

THE ABOVE 3 C'S WILL HELP AVOID SOME OTHER C'S. CONCUSSIONS—CRANIAL CATASTROPHIES---CONTUSIONS---COLLISIONS---CALAMITIES---CLUMSY

IN THE NORTHEAST ORTHOPEDICS IS A LUCRATIVE BUSINESS. HOW MUCH OF IT IS DUE TO SKIING?

FOR HERE THE P.C., --- POLITE CONSTRAINT

SILLY CON ALLEY

SILLY-CON-ALLEY

AS I LOOK AT THIS CARTOON, I ASK WHAT CAN IT BE ABOUT? COULD PLACES LIKE THIS EXIST? CABLE TELEVISION RECENTLY SHOWED A NUMBER OF STREET LIVING AREAS IN CALIFORNIA.

SILLY CON ALLEY

A SILLY CON ALLEY PROBABLY DOES EXIST. THERE ARE ALLEYS ALL OVER THE WORLD WITH MANY OF THEM POPULAR TOURIST PLACES.

IN NEW YORK CITY IN THE 1600S THROUGH THE 1700S MANY STREETS WERE CALLED ALLEYS BECAUSE THEY WERE VERY NARROW. SOME OF THEM STILL SHOW UP ON THE MAPS OF LOWER MANHATTAN.

THERE WAS EXCHANGE ALLEY DURING THE PETER STUYVESANT DAYS.

RYDERS ALLEY RENAMED EDENS ALLEY IS NEAR THE FULTON FISH MARKET.

THERE'S MECHANICS ALLEY NEAR THE MANHATTAN BRIDGE AND THE DOYER STREET ALLEY IN CHINATOWN.

WHEN WE WERE KIDS WE PLAYED IN AN ALLEY. NO CONS IN THIS ALLEY BUT AT TIMES THERE WERE SLEEPERS.

IF YOU EVER COME ACROSS AN ALLEY OCCUPIED BY SILLY CONS, IT COULD BECOME A TOURIST ATTRACTION.

THERE'S COMMUNITY P.C., --- PUBLIC CONCERN

77—BK AND BH, CANARY SWALLOWS THE CAT

BK AND BH RESPOND OUTRAGIOUSLY TO THE CAT AND THE CANARY PROVERB. THE 2 BIRDS KNOW THE BIGGEST CANARY CANNOT SWALLOW A CAT. THIS IS JUST TO FEEL THAT THEY CAN GET EVEN.

77—BK AND BH, CANARY SWALLOWS THE CAT

IT'S WRITTEN THAT CATS KILL A BILLION BIRDS EACH YEAR. WHEN BK AND BH HEAR THAT CAT WHO SWALLOWED THE CANARY PROVERB, IT UPSETS THEM.

PSYCHOLOGISTS SUPPLY REASONS WHY PEOPLE FEEL GOOD ABOUT GETTING REVENGE. WHAT A GOOD FEELING GETTING EVEN.

EVEN A MAKE BELIEVE GETTING EVEN THOUGHT MAKES ONE FEEL BETTER.

MAYBE GIVING THE BIRD HELPS DRIVERS GET BACK TO NORMAL DRIVING ACTIVITIES.

THERE ARE MANY REVENGE EXPRESSIONS,

REVENGE IS SWEET.

REVENGE FOR SOMETHING SMALL WILL RESULT IN BIGGER ONES.

BUT MAYBE, FORGIVENESS IS MORE REWARDING THAN REVENGE.

MAYBE THE BIRD SHOULD ONLY BE GIVEN AS A PET AND THAT BIRD SHOULD NOT BE GIVEN FROM ONE DRIVER TO ANOTHER DRIVER.

WE WANT P.C., PLEASANT COMMUNICATION

78—BEEKEE AND BILHORN, LOT'SA SEEDS

B AND B ARE TALKING ABOUT THE GRUB THEY LIKE THE BEST. MANY PUT VARIOUS BREAD PRODUCTS OUT FOR BIRD SURVIVAL. THE 2 BIRDS PREFER BAKERY RYE WITH PLENTY OF SEEDS.

78—BEEKEE AND BILHORN,   LOT'SA SEEDS

THERE ARE LISTS OF BIRDS AND THE FOODS THEY EAT. THE USUAL FOODS ARE SUNFLOWER SEEDS, SAFFLOWER SEEDS, CRACKED CORN, POPCORN, NUTS AND BERRIES.

BIRDS MAY EAT WORMS, BEETLES, SPIDERS AND INSECTS. IN ADDITION TO THESE LIVING DELICACIES, THEY EAT PEAS, OTHER VEGETABLE SCRAPS AND MEAT SCRAPS. BK AND BH NEVER LIKE EATING A BLOODY WORM. GIVE THEM THE USUAL SEEDS, BERRIES, NUTS, POPCORN, AND CANDIED POPCORN.

BEEKEE AND BILHORN OBSERVE PEOPLE EATING THOSE BIG HERO SANDWICHES BIGGER THAN BOTH BIRDS TOGETHER.

BEEKEE AND BILHORN ARE HAPPY EATING LIKE BIRDS.

79— SOMETHING TO SINK YOUR TEETH IN

SOMETHING TO SINK YOUR TEETH IN

THE TITLE SUGGESTS A PROJECT OR A CHORE THAT ONE GETS INVOLVED IN. YOU CAN SINK YOUR TEETH INTO THAT. BUT AS THE CARTOON SHOWS, THERE ARE PEOPLE WHO SINK THEIR TEETH INTO SOMETHING EVERY NIGHT.

79— SOMETHING TO SINK YOUR TEETH IN

THIS CARTOON BOOK IS SOMETHING I ENJOYED SINKING MY TEETH IN.

IF YOU THINK ABOUT IT THERE WOULD BE A NUMBER OF PROJECTS THAT YOU DIVED INTO, TEETH AND ALL.

REPAIRING A CAR, A HOME PROJECT OR SOMETHING TO DO WITH SCHOOL ARE ALL SINK YOUR TEETH IN STUFF.

RUNNING A MARATHON OR MAKING IT THROUGH A TRIATHALON GIVES BIG SATISFACTION WHEN ACCOMPLISHED.

FOR THIS TOONOLOGIST THE BEST SINKING MY TEETH IN EVENT IS A GOOD HERO SANDWICH.

THERE ARE SOME THAT USE THE GLASS OR DISH BECAUSE OF BEING INVOLVED IN AN ACCIDENT.

TODAY'S ATHLETES USE A MOUTH PIECE PROTECTING A PLAYER'S TEETH WHEN SMASHED IN THE MOUTH.

IT'S GOOD P.C.,   PREVENTING CRUNCH

Stool Pigeons

A PIGEON PLACED FIRMLY ON A TREE STUMP BECAME KNOWN AS A STOOL PIGEON. THE STOOL PIGEON WAS A DECOY TO GET HAWKS TO FLY INTO A NET. IN POLICE MOVIES THE STOOL PIGEON IS A DECOY OR INFORMER.

STOOL PIGEONS

STOOL PIGEONS WERE A BIG PART OF POLICE STORIES. THE DETECTIVE SHOWS AND MOVIES, SNEAKING IN A STOOL PIGEON PART, GAVE THE GOOD GUYS THE CLUES THAT HELPED SOLVE THE CRIME. SOME GREAT NAMES COME TO MIND.

THE GREAT ACTORS OF YEARS AGO LIKE CAGNEY, ROBINSON, DURYEA. BOGART, ANDREWS AND LORRE WOULD HAVE THE STOOLIE TALK.

DO YOU REMEMBER SAM SPADE, PHILIP MARLOWE, MIKE HAMMER AND OTHER MOVIE DETECTIVES?

THE ORIGINAL STOOL PIGEONS, REAL PIGEONS SERVED THE PURPOSE OF DECOY, FASTENED TO A TREE OR SOMETHING LIKE A STOOL. ITS PREDATOR WAS TRICKED AND CAPTURED.

ALTHOUGH IT'S PROBABLY THE SAME, STOOL PIGEON SOUNDS BETTER THAN TATTLETALE AND SNITCH.

THIS IS P.C., PIGEON COOPERATION

81—NEWS, 2017, CONGRESS HAD HANDS FULL

2017 CONGRESS HAD A NUMBER OF IMPORTANT ISSUES TO STRUGGLE WITH. AND THEY DID STRUGGLE.
REPLACE A SUPREME COURT JUSTICE.
CONFIRM A NEW CABINET AND DEAL WITH REPEAL OF THE HEALTH CARE LAW.

81—NEWS, 2017 CONGRESS HAD HANDS FULL

IN 2017 CONGRESS WAS PRESENTED WITH MANY CONTROVERSIAL ISSUES.

BORDER SECURITY

CONSTRUCTION OF A WALL

IMMIGRATION LAWS

ELECTION TAMPERING

CONFIRMING CABINET MEMBERS

$$$$$$$ APPROPRIATION FOR MILITARY

INFRASTRUCTURE IMPROVEMENT

CITIZEN SAFETY

TAX REFORM LAWS

CONFIRMATION OF JUDGES

CONGRESS ALSO HAD AN ISSUE WITH SOME MEMBERS' DISRESPECTFUL TREATMENT OF WOMEN.

AS YOU CAN SEE, CONGRESS HAD ITS HANDS FULL.

TRY TO BE P.C., PROPER CONDUCT

82—NEWS, A SIDE OF THE AISLE

THEIR SIDE OF THE AISLE IS THE BACKSIDE

LABELS, LABELS, LABELS, THAT'S WHAT YOU GET FROM NEWS STATIONS. RIGHT WING, RIGHT SIDE, LEFT WING, LEFT SIDE, CONSERVATIVE, LIBERAL, WITH THESE WORDS THEY DESCRIBE PEOPLE. THEY ALL SEEM TO HAVE A FAVORITE SIDE(OF THE AISLE).

82—NEWS, A SIDE OF THE AISLE

ACCORDING TO THE PERSON'S LABEL, WHO AND HOW THEY VOTE CAN BE PREDICTED. ALSO YOU KNOW WHICH TELEVISION NEWS STATION THEY WATCH.

ACCORDING TO A PERSON'S LABEL, YOU KNOW WHICH T.V. PERSONALITY THEY TUNE TO BECAUSE THE PERSONALITY ALSO WEARS A LABEL.

THE LABELS REPRESENT THE 2 POLITICAL PARTIES.

ONE SIDE OF THE AISLE USES THEIR SET OF WORDS AND THE OTHER SIDE HAS AN OPPOSITE SET.

WHEN MOST APPEAR ON T.V. YOU KNOW WHAT THEY WILL SAY ALMOST WORD FOR WORD.

THE RHETORIC CAN BECOME ANNOYING.

SOME GUY ENJOYED ANNOYING PEOPLE. WHEN THEY SHOWED DISPLEASURE HE WOULD REMARK, TOUCHY, TOUCHY. THESE CARTOONS ARE REMINDERS OF HIS WORDS TOUCHY, TOUCHY.

ONLY WAY THIS IS P.C., PERSONALLY CAUSTIC

83—BEEKEE AND BILHORN, IT TAKES BOTH WINGS

BK AND BH HAVE BEEN FOLLOWING CONGRESS. THEY OBSERVE THAT THE LEFT WING AND RIGHT WING CANNOT COORDINATE. THE 2 BIRDS WANT TO TELL CONGRESS, IT TAKES BOTH WINGS TO FLY.

83—BEEKEE AND BILHORN, IT TAKES BOTH WINGS

B AND B REMEMBER THERE WAS A LAW PASSED WITH ONLY LEFT WING VOTES, ZERO RIGHT WINGING. MORE RECENTLY THERE WAS A LAW PASSED BY THE RIGHT WING WITH BIG TIME NO VOTES FROM THE LEFT WINGERS.

BEEKEE AND BILHORN LOOK FOR THE 2 WINGS TO WORK TOGETHER SO THAT THINGS CAN GET OFF THE GROUND. SO FAR ONLY THE LIPS ARE FLAPPING, CALLING EACH OTHER INSULTING NAMES.

THE BEST IS WHEN THE NAME CALLING BEGINS, MY FRIEND ON THE OTHER SIDE IS VERY MUCH A BIGOT, EXTREMIST, HYPOCRITE, ZEALOT, RACIST, SHILL, MISOGYNIST, DEPLORABLE, PUPPET, UNFIT, LIAR AND WACKO AND THAT'S JUST THE START. THE INSULTS ARE TOSSED BACK AND FORTH.

THE 2 BIRDS ARE WAITING FOR WORDS BIRDBRAIN, DO-DO BIRD OR SOME ANGRY SENATORS GIVING EACH OTHER, THE BIRD.

84—BEEKEE AND BILHORN, A DROP OVER

THE 2 BIRDS HAVE A TREAT WHEN THERE'S A BALLGAME IN TOWN. THE POPCORN AND CRACKERJACKS THAT WIND UP ON THE SEATS AND GROUND MAKE A FEAST FOR THE BIRDS.

84—BEEKEE AND BILHORN, A DROP OVER

OFTEN BIRDS LIKE GATHERING ON THE TOP OF THE STADIUM WHILE A GAME IS PLAYED.

IS IT POSSIBLE THEY LIKE THE CHEERING OR THE SINGING?

BEEKEE LIKES THE SONG TAKE ME OUT TO THE BALLGAME. BH LIKES TO TELL THE BIRDS, THE WORDS WERE WRITTEN BY JACK NORWORTH, THEN ALBERT VON TILZER PUT THE WORDS TO MUSIC. THE SONG GOES BACK TO 1908 AND WAS INSPIRED WHEN MR. NORWORTH WENT PAST THE POLO GROUNDS BASEBALL PARK, OF NEW YORK CITY.

BOTH OF THE SONGWRITERS HAD NEVER BEEN TO A BASEBALL GAME BEFORE THEY WROTE THE SONG.

BEEKEE LIKES TO TWEET TAKE ME OUT TO THE BALLGAME, WHILE FLYING AROUND DURING THE SEVENTH INNING STRETCH.

85—BEEKEE AND BILHORN,   BIRD BOOK, LADYBIRD

PEOPLE WITH BIRD NAMES WILL BE FEATURED IN BILHORN'S BIRD BOOK. THE BOOK WILL PROMOTE THE GREAT THINGS DONE BY THEM.

85—BEEKEE AND BILHORN, BIRD BOOK, LADYBIRD LADYBIRD WILL BE GLORIFIED AS A MAKE AMERICA BEAUTIFUL ADVOCATE.

LIKE ALL BIRDS, SHE FAVORED PLANTING MORE FLOWERS.

THE HIGHWAY BEAUTIFICATION ACT WAS CALLED LADYBIRD'S BILL.

QUAYLE WAS AN ADVOCATE FOR NASA FLYING INTO SPACE.

THE SPELLING FOR THE BIRD IS QUAIL. IT IS A NESTING BIRD IN THE PHEASANT FAMILY, MAKING IT A GAMEBIRD. V. P. QUAYLE WAS ALSO A FREQUENT TARGET.

THERE ARE SO MANY ROBINS TO WRITE ABOUT. THEY WOULD FILL MORE THAN ONE BOOK. THERE ARE MANY ATHLETES, SHOW PEOPLE AND OTHERS?

HOW MANY FAMOUS ROBINS CAN YOU NAME?

ALWAYS THINKING

THE DISCUSSION TOPIC FOR THIS MEETING WAS IMMIGRATION POLICIES. MAYBE THE WALL AND DACA ISSUES COULD BE SOLVED. TOONS THINKS THAT A MORE FUN ISSUE FOR SOME OF THEM WOULD BE TAX COLLECTING METHODS.

ALWAYS THINKING

THERE IS NO DOUBT THERE WILL BE $$$$$$$$ MADE OPENING A BUSINESS AT THE WALL. THERE WILL BE FEES TO SEE THE WALL, FEES TO TOUCH THE WALL, FEES TO PASS THROUGH THE WALL, FEES TO LOOK OVER THE WALL AND A FEE TO CLIMB THE WALL. THERE ARE THESE TYPE FEES ALL OVER, YOU'VE PAID PARKING FEES, PARK ENTRANCE FEES, LOOK THROUGH THE TELESCOPE FEES AND BEACH FEES. NOW BEING CONSIDERED IS A FEE TO ENTER MIDTOWN MANHATTAN. ONE DAY YOU WILL BE WEIGHED AND MEASURED TO DETERMINE YOUR FEE TO BE ALLOWED TO WALK AROUND TIMES SQUARE. SO FAR THE POLITICIANS ARE NOT THE BEST PROBLEM SOLVERS, BUT TERRIFIC AT FINDING WAYS TAXING CITIZENS.

DO YOU LIKE P.C.?   PROMOTING   CASH

87-- THEY KNEED TO PROTEST

IN 1773 THERE WAS A POLITICAL PROTEST. THE BOSTON TEA PARTY ATTRACTED A GROUP OF PATRIOTS TO PUT ON KNEE PADS AND TAKE SOME TEA. IT DIDN'T HAPPEN THAT WAY, BUT THERE WAS A PROTEST.

87-- THEY KNEED TO PROTEST

THE KNEED TO PROTEST PROTESTORS ARE MUCH IMPROVED OVER THE TEA PARTY PROTESTORS.

THE BOSTON TEA PARTYERS WERE QUITE ACTIVE.

THE KNEED TO PROTESTORS JUST STAYED IN ONE PLACE, USING KNEE PADS NOT TO HURT THEIR KNEES.

AFTER THE PROTEST THEY STOOD LOOKING TO PLAY A GAME.

THE PROTESTORS SHOULD HAVE HELD A CUP OF TEA THAT WOULD REPRESENT SOMETHING.

THEIR PROTEST COULD INVOLVE A SLOGAN ACTIVELY ANNOUNCING AND ALSO OFFERING A SOLUTION TO THE ISSUE PROTESTED. WHEN YOU KNEED TO PROTEST, HOW ABOUT A TALL SIGN AND STAND TALL OFFERING A BETTER VIEW OF THE ISSUE.

PERFECT P.C., POLITICAL CLASH

88—NEWS, NO GOLDEN GRAB

THE NEWSTOON POINTS TO THE BLACK EYE GIVEN TO THE MOVIE INDUSTRY WHEN MISCONDUCT BECAME THE PREVALENT ISSUE ON TELEVISION.

88-- NEWS,   NO GOLDEN GRAB

IS IT JUST POOR MANNERS OR IS IT WORSE?

WITH ALL THE RECENT PUBLICITY IT SEEMS THAT THIS BEHAVIOR WILL NO LONGER BE KEPT UNDER RAPS.

EVERY INDUSTRY INCLUDING GOVERNMENT AGENCIES ARE PAYING STRICT ATTENTION TO THIS TYPE OF M I S S BEHAVIOR.

THIS STUFF IS NOW FRONT AND CENTER IN PEOPLE'S MINDS, WHERE IN THE PAST IT WAS ON THE REAR BURNER.

IN THE PAST ONLY SOME THOUGHT THE SITUATION WAS WELL IN HAND, NOW IT SEEMS THAT PEOPLE HAVE A BETTER GRIP ON IT.

THIS NEWSTOON NEEDS CHANGE TO BE P.C., PREVENTING CAROUSING

ICONS REFER TO PEOPLE ON THE TOP RUNG, WELL RESPECTED IN THEIR FIELD. HERE ARE 3 CONS WITH NAMES THAT BEGIN WITH THE LETTER I.

3 I CONS

THERE ARE MANY ICONS THAT WIND UP IN THE CLINK. SOME FROM THE INVESTMENT BUSINESS, SOME ARE POLITICIANS AND SOME REAL ESTATE DEALERS ARE FOUND TO BE GUILTY OF SOME ILLEGAL OFFENSES.

THESE 3 GUYS BOUGHT A LITTLE CANDY STORE WHERE THEY WANTED TO BE ICONS IN THE NUMBERS AND BOOKIE BUSINESS.

THEY WERE GIVEN INSTRUCTIONS ON RUNNING A CANDY STORE. THEY ORDERED THE NEWSPAPERS, ICE CREAM, CANDY, SODA AND THE REST. THEY ROTATED GETTING UP EARLY IN THE MORNING TO DEAL WITH THE PAPERS AND THE EARLY MORNING CUSTOMERS. THEY BEGAN DOING VERY WELL IN THE GAMBLING END.

AFTER A SHORT TIME, THEY DIDN'T GET THE STORE OPEN EARLY. THEY ALLOWED PEOPLE TO TAKE NEWSPAPERS WITHOUT PAYING. THEY LIKED THE BETTING BUSINESS, BUT HAD NO INTEREST IN THE PENNY AND DIME BUSINESS. IF A KID BOUGHT CANDY AND NEEDED CHANGE, THE CANDY WAS FREE. KIDS KNEW BUYING CANDY COST A DIME, AND IF THEY OFFERED A QUARTER OR A DOLLAR, THEY WOULD BE TOLD TAKE THE CANDY. KIDS LEARNED HOW TO GET FREE CANDY AT TIMES.

SOME MONTHS LATER, THE STORE WAS CLOSED.

NOW FIGURE OUT THE END OF THE 3 I CONS STORY.

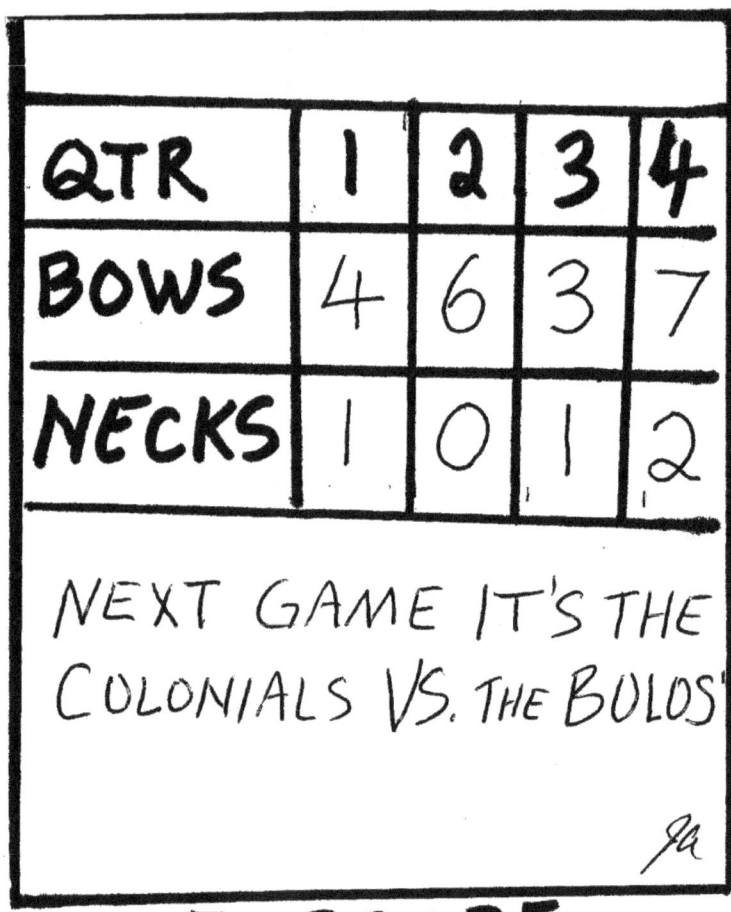

THIS CARTOON APPEARED IN THE JUNIOR HIGH SCHOOL NEWSPAPER. THAT SHOULD BE ITS LEVEL. BUT WHEN A TEACHER ASKED, HOW IS THIS A TIE SCORE WITH THOSE NUMBERS? THIS CARTOON BECAME A CARTOON FOR ALL AGES.

TIE SCORE

AFTER THE TEACHER'S QUESTION ABOUT TIE SCORE, THIS CARTOON BECAME A GOTCHA TOON. JUST LIKE THE YANKEE SCORE COULD HAVE DIFFERENT NUMBERS, THIS TIE SCORE DOESN'T NEED TO BE A TIE.

IT IS THE HOPE OF THE TOONOLOGIST THAT THERE'S HUMOR THROUGHOUT THIS BOOK ABSORBED BY THE READERS.

LET'S STRESS THIS IS A CARTOON BOOK. SOME CARTOONS PROMOTE SERIOUS ISSUES. TIE SCORE IS NOT SERIOUS IN ANY WAY. THAT'S WHY IT'S A FUN FOR ALL CARTOON.

USING THE TOONS, SERIOUS CAN BE TURNED TO HUMOR WHILE HUMOR CAN BE TURNED TO SERIOUS.

IF THIS HAPPENS THE BOOK IS A SUCCESS.

WHY IS THIS P.C.? --- PRECOCIOUS CLARITY

91—NEWS,   WALLA,DACA,CHAINA

WALLA, DACA, CHAINA

WILL THE WALL STAND TALL, LISTEN TO PEOPLE DEBATE,
WILL THEY DECIDE
OR WILL THEY PLAY, WAIT, WAIT, WAIT?

91—NEWS,   WALLA, DACA, CHAINA

THEY DEBATE IN CONGRESS   THEY DEBATE ON T.V.

THEY DEBATE ACCORDING TO THEIR GROUP

THEY DEBATE AND THEN THEY FLEE

WHO WANTS A WALL   WHO WANTS A WALL TO FALL

WHO WANTS DACA TO BE STANDING TALL

WHO LIKES IT BEST WHEN IT'S AT A CRAWL

THE WORDS GO BACK AND FORTH

ALMOST LIKE A ROCKING HORSE

SOMETIMES THE WORDS HAVE THOUGHT

SOMETIMES THE WORDS ARE COARSE

AT SOME POINT THEY SHOULD END THE STALL

HAVE A SOLUTION WITH SOME AGREEMENT FOR ALL.

WALLA, DACA, CHAINA 2018

TO BE P.C.,   PATRIOTIC COURAGE

THE MEETING OF INFLUENTIAL PEOPLE WAS TELEVISED. GREAT MINDS COULD OFFER IDEAS AND SOLUTIONS. BUT, SOMETIMES THE MEETING ENDS WITH WHAT, WHERE, WHO AND HOW?

92—NEWS, WHAT, WHERE, WHO

A TEACHER'S TEST QUESTION READ, FILL IN THE
CORRECT ANSWER. ____? ___? ____? ____ IS THE
VICE PRESIDENT OF THE UNITED STATES OF AMERICA?
9 STUDENTS FILLED IN "WHO" FOR THE ANSWER.
IF THOSE GATHERED FOR SOLUTIONS RESPONDED
WITH WHO, WHERE, WHAT, DO THEY GET CREDIT?
THE ISSUES HAVE RAISED QUESTIONS.
WHY SEPARATE PEOPLE WITH A WALL?
AREN'T ALL PEOPLE HUMAN BEINGS?
WHY CAN'T THEY BE PUT AT THE HEAD OF THE LIST?
WHY PUT THEM AT THE HEAD OF THE LIST?
WHY SHOULD FAMILIES BE SEPARATED?
MUST THEY REMAIN TOGETHER FOREVER?
WHERE IS THE TOGETHER PLACE?
HOW FAR APART WILL THEY BE ALLOWED TO LIVE?
SHOULDN'T THEY BE REPRESENTED IN CONGRESS?
ARE NON-CITIZENS REPRESENTED IN CONGRESS?
HOW SHOULD LAW BREAKERS BE TREATED?
AREN'T THEY NEEDED FOR FARMS AND MILITARY?
THE QUESTIONS KEEP FLOWING, WHILE HOPING FOR
SOME SOLUTIONS.

THIS IS P.C., POLITICAL CONFLICT

WATCHING ONES ASS IS STAYING AWAY FROM TROUBLE. COVERING YOUR ASS IS THE ATTEMPT TO REMOVE SUSPICION. THIS GUY WANTS NO TROUBLE, HE'S JUST WATCHING HIS DONKEY.

93-- WATCHING HIS ASS

ONE PLACE WHERE YOU CAN'T COVER YOUR ASS AND AT THE SAME TIME EVERYONE ELSE CAN WATCH YOUR ASS IS WHEN YOU PUT ON THOSE HOSPITAL GOWNS.

WHEN THE OPENING IS IN THE BACK, COVERING YOUR ASS IS OUT OF THE GAME.

WHEN YOU BEND OVER YOU CAN'T WATCH YOUR ASS, B U T T EVERYONE TO YOUR REAR CAN.

TOONS SUGGESTS A PONCHO TYPE GOWN WITH PLENTY OF FLARE. WHEN WEARING, IT WOULD COVER IT ALL. IT CAN BE LIFTED FOR COMPLETE ACCESS. YOU WOULD NOT NEED TO BE CONCERNED WITH PEEKS AT YOUR DONKEY.

MAYBE LIKE THE GUY IN THE CARTOON, YOU GET A SIGN SAYING DON'T LOOK AT MY DONKEY.

THE SIGN WILL BE P.C., PRIVATE CONTENTS

WATER UNDER THE BRIDGE

AN OFTEN USED RESPONSE OR THOUGHT. IT HAPPENED, IT WAS VERY BAD BUT IT CANNOT BE ALTERED, SO IT'S BEST TO MOVE ON. IT'S WATER UNDER THE BRIDGE.

94-- WATER UNDER THE BRIDGE

AFTER EVERY GAME WIN OR LOSE, NEWS PEOPLE INTERVIEW THE COACH. WHEN THERE WAS A LOSS, IT'S WE PLAYED HARD BUT NOT ENOUGH TO WIN. THIS ONE IS BEHIND US. THE NEXT DAY WHEN THE LOSS IS BIGGER, IT WAS NOT ENOUGH OFFENSE, TODAYS GAME IS IN THE PAST, WE MOVE ON. LIKE THE CARTOON SAYS,

IT'S WATER UNDER THE BRIDGE.

THE NEXT WATER UNDER THE BRIDGE STORY IS HEARTBREAKING. AFTER THE RAIN DISASTERS IN 2017, THE WORST HIT VICTIMS WIND UP ON THE NEWS. PEOPLE LOST THEIR HOMES AND MOST OF THEIR POSSESSIONS. THEY ARE DEPENDING ON INSURANCE $$$$$ TO GET BACK ON THEIR FEET.

THE RESPONSE TO NEWS QUESTIONS, IT'S A TRAGEDY, THERE WAS NO DEFENSE, WE MUST LOOK TO RECOOP.

IN HOUSTON THEY STOCKED UP WITH FOOD AND WATER, PLUS A BIG GENERATOR. THEY FELT SECURE WITH THE RAINFALL. THE NEXT MORNING, THEY WATCHED THE SHOES FLOATING BY THE DOOR. NOON TIME THE WATER LEVEL WAS AT THEIR WAISTLINE AND THEY WERE EVACUATED TO A DRYER AREA. IT WAS DAYS BEFORE THEY COULD RETURN AND ASSESS THE DAMAGE. THEY WERE ABLE TO REBUILD WHILE OTHERS HAD TO MOVE ON.

SO MANY WATER UNDER THE BRIDGE STORIES.

                P. C.,   PERSERVERING COMPASSION

WE ARE VS. PROFILING

WE ARE AGAINST PROFILING.

YOU SEE THE PROFILING THAT THESE GUYS ARE AGAINST. THEY SHOULD NOT BE VS. PROFILING. REMEMBER THE GREAT JIMMY DURANTE, WHEN HE DISPLAYED HIS SHNOZZ AND TALENT MAKING HIM ONE OF THE GREAT SHOW BUSINESS STARS.

95-- WE ARE VS. PROFILING

PROFILING IS A BIG SOCIAL AND LEGAL ISSUE.

AFTER A MASS MURDER PEOPLE ARE ASKED IF THEY SAW ANYTHING SUSPICIOUS ABOUT THE MURDERER. THEY SAY YES, BUT THEY WOULD NOT WANT TO PROFILE. IF YOU PROFILE YOU COULD BE ACCUSED OF PROFILING THEN THE GROUPS WILL PROFILE YOU AS A PROFILER. THE POLICE ARE TOLD NOT TO PROFILE. SO IF A TALL THIN DRIVER IS PULLED OVER FOR SPEEDING, NEXT TO BE PULLED OVER WOULD BE A SHORT FAT SPEEDER. GOING AFTER THE SAME TYPE, THAT'S PROFILING.

LICENSE PLATES WILL INDICATE THE SIZE AND OTHER SPECIFICS OF THE DRIVERS. THERE WOULD BE ONE COLOR PLATE FOR HEAVIES, ANOTHER COLOR PLATE FOR SKINNY AND SHORT. GO AFTER ONE OF EACH.

IF THEY TICKET SOMEONE WITH A LICENSE, NEXT TO BE PULLED OVER MUST BE SOMEONE WITH NO LICENSE.

THERE'S NOTHING LIKE A GOOD PROFILING PROGRAM TO KEEP THE CITIZENS UNDER CONTROL.

THESE GUYS ARE RIGHT ON, DO NOT PICK ON 3 GUYS WITH PROTRUDING NOSES IN THE SAME DAY.

IT IS P. C., --- PROTRUDING CONSTRAINT

THE WISHEE WASHEE WISH

THIS IS THE LAST ROUNDTABLE NEWSTOON. IN THE PREVIOUS FIVE THERE WERE NO CONCRETE SOLUTIONS TO THE MAIN ISSUES. IN THE SIXTH ROUNDTABLE NEWSTOON, THE GROUP LOOKS FOR IMPEACHMENT.

96--NEWS, WISHEE, WASHEE, WISH

REMEMBER THE FIRST 5 ROUNDTABLE TOONS?
IN #1, THE MAIN HOPE WAS THAT MEXICAN FOOD WOULD BE ALLOWED IN THROUGH THE BORDER.
TOON #4, THE OPPOSITION WAS HOPING TO REMOVE THE WALL FOR SHOVEL READY JOBS.
ROUNDTABLE TOON #18, MANY QUESTIONS ARE BROUGHT UP ABOUT THE WALL, ABOUT DACA AND ABOUT KEEPING YOUR DOCTOR.
IN #86, POLITICIANS ARE HOPING TO MAKE $$$$$ BY SETTING UP TOLLS ALONG THE WALL.
IN #92, THE COMBATANTS ARE FIRING QUESTIONS, RATHER THAN SOLUTIONS.
TOON #96 FOCUSES ON THE IMPEACHMENT INFANTRY. THE ARMY OF POLITICIANS, ACTORS, PROFESSORS AND STUDENTS ALTERNATE FLIPPING GRENADES IN CONGRESS, SMOKE BOMBS ON TELEVISION AND MUD AT THE WALL.
THIS NEWSTOON POINTS OUT THE WISH FOR IMPEACHMENT IS STILL ON THEIR TABLE.

P. C., PEACHY CONGRESS

WON BY A HARE

ANOTHER HOMONYM WINDS UP A CARTOON IN THIS BOOK. THE IDIOM OR PROVERB MADE THIS ONE EASY. IT WASN'T A RABBIT THAT WON THE RACE, IT WAS WON BY THE BIGGER, STRONGER AND FASTER HARE.

WON BY A HARE

RABBITS AND HARE ARE IN THE SAME FAMILY CALLED LEPORIDAE.

RABBITS BUILD A HOME IN THE GROUND, LIVING IN A GROUP.

HARE BUILD A NEST IN THE GRASS ABOVE GOUND. WHEN FEELING DANGER THE HARE RUNS AWAY WHILE THE RABBITS TRY TO HIDE.

RABBITS ARE BORN BLIND AND NO FUR, HARE HAVE OPEN EYES AND HAIR OR FUR AT BIRTH.

THE MOST POPULAR RABBIT OR HARE IS BUGS BUNNY. IN MOVIES BUGS COULD DO THINGS THAT ARE TRAITS OF THE HARE. BUGS WAS FAST AND TOUGH. SUCH GREAT MEMORIES OF THOSE WONDERFUL CARTOONS.

THIS RACE WAS WON BY A HARE AND NOT BY A HAIR.

IT CAN BE P. C.,   PLEASANT   CARTOON

WORKING IN A CLIP JOINT

WORKING IN A **CLIP JOINT**

IN BROOKLYN WHEN A BUSINESS IS UNDERHANDED, THEY LABEL IT A CLIP JOINT. HERE A PLACE SELLING ALL TYPE OF CLIPS IS LABELED A CLIP JOINT.

WORKING IN A CLIP JOINT

WHEN YOU GO TO AN ALL YOU CAN EAT PLACE, IF THE SERVER DOESN'T RETURN AFTER YOU ORDERED TWICE, YOU WERE PROBABLY AT A CLIP JOINT.

THERE ARE STORES THAT SELL FOR GOOD PRICES. IF YOU ARE NOT TOLD YOU ARE BUYING DISCONTINUED OR LAST YEARS MODELS, IT MIGHT BE A CLIP JOINT.

A FRIEND ENJOYED PUTTING STORE BRAND LIQUORS IN HIGH END BOTTLES, WATCHING THE DRINKERS THINKING THAT THEY ARE ENJOYING THE BEST.

SOME SAY LESSER QUALITY LIQUORS ARE SUBSTITUTED FOR TOP BRANDS IN MANY RESTAURANTS AND BARS, IF THIS IS TRUE THEY SPENT THEIR $$$ IN A CLIP JOINT.

THE BARBER SHOP IS NOT THE ONLY PLACE YOU CAN GET CLIPPED.

IT WOULD BE P. C., --- PAINFULLY CLIPPED

99-- BEEKEE AND BILHORN, FOWL PLAY MISSING

WE SPOKE ABOUT A FOWL PLAY CARTOON. TURKEY PLAYING SOCCER COULD BE FUN. IT WASN'T DONE. WOULD YOU LIKE DOING ONE?

99--BEEKEE AND BILHORN,   FOWL PLAY MISSING

A BASEBALL CARTOON WITH FOWL COULD HIT ON 2 POSSIBILITIES.

FOWL PLAYING AND RUNNING IN THE FOUL LINES.

HOW ABOUT FOWL INTERACTION WITH THE FOUL POLES?

THE BIRDS PLAYING SOCCER WOULD BE FUN.

A BIRD KICKING A FOOTBALL THROUGH THE GOALPOST WOULD WORK.

OF COURSE, THERE WOULD BE SOME COMMENTARY RELATING TO THE TOON.

BEEKEE AND BILHORN ARE QUESTIONING THE NEED FOR MORE BIRDTOONS PUT IN THIS BOOK.

IF YOU WOULD LIKE MORE BIRDTOONS YOU CAN SCRATCH OUT A COUPLE AND ADD THEM TO THE BOOK.

100—BEEKEE AND BILHORN, MORE BIRDS?

THERE ARE NOW 100 CARTOONS, ¼ OF THEM ARE BIRDTOONS.
THE 2 BIRDS AGREE THAT MORE BIRDTOONS IS UNADVISABLE.

100—BEEKEE AND BILHORN, MORE BIRDS?

BEEKEE AND BILHORN COVERED PLENTY OF TOPICS: TWEETING, CURRENT EVENTS, TAX PLAN, NEST EGG, FLU SHOT, HISTORY, HENRY, JONES, AND PUTNAM, BIRD PROVERBS, 2 BIRDS WITH 1 STONE, THE CAT AND THE CANARY AND GIVING PEOPLE THE BIRD.

THE BIRDBOOK FEATURED F. NIGHTINGALE, BLUEBIRD THE PIRATE, LADYBIRD, BIRD MUSIC AND MOVIES.

THE 2 BIRDS WERE HAPPY TO EXPLAIN WHAT THEY SAW FROM ABOVE.

AT TIMES THE 2 BIRDS HAVE OFFBEAT THOUGHTS. THEY KNOW WHEN WAITING FOR A DOCTOR'S EXAM, YOU CAN BE TOLD THE DOCTOR WILL BE WITH YOU SHORTLY. THEY ASK WHY AT THE DENTIST YOU ARE TOLD THE DOCTOR WILL BE IN SHORTLY. WHY NOT THE DENTIST OR THE PSYCHOLOGIST WILL SEE YOU. SOMETIMES BIRDS ARE MORE INTERESTING THAN ???

IT'S TOP SHELF BECAUSE WITH 101 TOONS, THERE'S COMMENTARY FOR EACH TOON. COMMENTARY PROVIDING EDUCATION, HUMOR AND CONFUSION.

101-- THIS BOOK IS TOP SHELF

THE CARTOONS CAME FROM ALL DIRECTIONS, FRONT, THE BACK AND OUT OF LEFTFIELD. YOU PROBABLY GOT TO LIKE THE 2 BIRDS AND THEIR THOUGHTS. THEY ARE DEFINITELY WELL ROUNDED WITH MANY INTERESTS. THE NEWSTOONS OFFERED CONGRESS IN-ACTION. CONGRESS AVOIDING IMPORTANT ISSUES IN 2017. MANY NEWSTOONS FOCUSED ON THE 2017 HARRASSING WOMEN ISSUE, WHICH WAS SHARED BY POLITICIANS AND HOLLYWOOD. IN ADDITION TO THE BIRDTOONS AND NEWSTOONS ARE SPICETOONS, SAYINGS, PROVERBS, IDIOMS, CASUAL AND EXPRESSIONS. THE WRITING WITH THE CARTOONS SHOWS A PICTURE CAN RESULT IN VARIED THOUGHTS.

MY 14 FAVORITE SPICE CARTOONS ARE:

BOARD DRY
CHANGING POLES
A DOG POUND
GETTING A LEG UP
HE BED VETS
HOME SCHOOLING
IT'S CASE BY CASE
A REAR STEAK
LONELY AT THE TOP
PROOF'S IN THE PUDDING
THE PROTESTEES
A ROYAL FLUSH
SINK YOUR TEETH
TIE SCORE
WE ARE VS. PROFILING

THERE'S ONE FOR GOOD LUCK, & GOOD LUCK TO YOU.

REMEMBER P. C.,   PROMOTE CARTOONS

THE TOONOLOGIST THANKS THE 2 BIRDS, THE SENATE, THE HOUSE OF REPRESENTATIVES AND THE GAGGLE OF CHARACTERS THAT CAUSED THIS CREATIVE CRANIUM TO CONCOCT THESE CARTOONS. THE TOONOLOGIST'S OBJECTIVE IS COMEDIC CANDOR TO ENTERTAIN AND STIMULATE CONVERSATION

101 CARTOONS • BIRDTOONS • NEWSTOONS
101 CARTOONS © 2018
J. ASCHER

www.ingramcontent.com/pod-product-compliance
Lightning Source LLC
Chambersburg PA
CBHW071435080526
44587CB00014B/1858